# Mentoring with Morgan

# Mentoring with Morgan

KAREN SCHLACK

*Foreword by Alton B. Pollard III*

WIPF & STOCK · Eugene, Oregon

MENTORING WITH MORGAN

Wipf & Stock
An Imprint of Wipf and Stock Publishers
199 W. 8th Ave., Suite 3
Eugene, OR 97401

www.wipfandstock.com

PAPERBACK ISBN: 978-1-7252-6488-5
HARDCOVER ISBN: 978-1-7252-6489-2
EBOOK ISBN: 978-1-7252-6490-8

Manufactured in the U.S.A.   08/11/20

For Daniel, my beloved husband,
who has always supported this book
and patiently provided technical support
and videos of live sermons.

# Contents

# Sermon Videos

*https://mentoringwithmorgan.com/resources/*

*Chapter 8*
"Like Those Who Dream"

*Chapter 10*
"Hold On"

*Chapter 11*
"An Unhindered Kingdom"

*Chapter 13*
"The Gift of Diversity"

*Chapter 14*
"Work to Do"
"Always Remembered"

# Sermon Manuscripts

*https:// mentoringwithmorgan.com/resources*

*Chapter 4*
"Back to Normal"
"Rachael Weeping"

*Chapter 5*
"Kept in Unity"

*Chapter 6*
"Love is Patient"

*Chapter 7*
"Welcome to Luke"
"In the Season of Our Hatred"

*Chapter 8*
"Like Those Who Dream"

*Chapter 10*
"Hold On"

# Acknowledgments

*A great cloud of witnesses has carried me on their shoulders to the place where I now stand . . . book in hand. After writing the early drafts of the manuscript, the following persons read the manuscript and offered comments, corrections, and encouragement:*

Karla Bellinger

Lant and Amanda Davis

Margaret Grau

Jan Van Lear

Cally McKinney

Chris Palmquist

Alton Pollard

Dorothy Ridings

Judy Ryan

Daniel Schlack

Katie Shaw-Thompson

Lynne Smith

Pat Somers

Debby Walters

*Also heartfelt thanks to:*

My patient and talented husband Daniel, who filmed my sermons for over five years and provided technical assistance during the preparation of this book.

Mathan Chakarabarthi and Ian Miska for website design.

Louisville Seminary, a faithful seed bed (seminary) for me, providing provocative instruction and most of all, Morgan Roberts! Morgan carried my seminary education for fifteen years beyond my graduation. The seminary was also a receptive place when I first introduced this book to them during the President's Roundtable in 2019.

First Presbyterian Church in Elgin, Illinois, full of faithful listeners to my sermons, week after week. They provided the context for my journey. The choir, the Sunday school, the session, and each member gave me their love and shared the precious moments of their lives with me.

Holy Wisdom Monastery in Middleton, Wisconsin, the place that provided a space for me to write and retreat. The prayerful, peaceful, and beautiful monastery grounds were the place I made the decision to write the book and the place where I wrote many of the words in this book.

# Foreword:
# The Music God Hears

There is in every person that which waits, waits,
waits and listens for the sound of the genuine in herself. There is that in every person that waits—waits
and listens—for the sound of the genuine in other
people. And when these two sounds come together,
this is the music God heard when God said, "let us
make humankind in our image."[1]

The world ever stands in need of good preaching. In this gem of a
book, two ministers—one a fledgling preacher, the other a seasoned
pastor, both of whose hearts hunger for God—take us on a me-
lodic journey through fifteen years of sermonic inspiration, social
engagement, self-discovery, and disclosure. The sacred saturates
every page.

I first met Karen Schlack less than two years ago when she
served on the presidential search committee for Louisville Presbyterian Theological Seminary. Hers was an attentive and inviting
presence then. At present a member of our President's Roundtable,

1. Thurman, "Sound of the Genuine," 14–15.

she remains so still. This year, I was honored to spend time with celebrated pastor emeritus F. Morgan Roberts. I look forward to doing so again.

Reflecting on my own years of formation, I found a deep resonance with many of the experiences and insights shared by Karen and Morgan. *Mentoring with Morgan* is a compact tome and substantial testimony. It offers the reader-listener a litany of biblical, theological, and ethical insights, harmonic language, and homiletical wisdom.

The stories shared about sermon preparation and mentoring response accompany life's passages for the two authors. Their stories intersect at Louisville Presbyterian Theological Seminary as student and esteemed staff member. It is a covenantal relationship that continued to flourish cross-country, through weekly emails, by phone, and more. We journey with them, chapter by chapter, through techniques of sermon preparation and delivery, out into the daily walk of life.

More than a manual on preaching, Karen and Morgan present a thoughtful and captivating dialogue that grapples with the dilemmas, contradictions, and joys of the preaching moment. Creating what they have called the "mentoring room," in which the give-and-take of insights is shared, they faithfully discuss a range of issues from preaching without a manuscript to social justice engagement and the transition to life as a retiring pastor.

The sermons Karen shares in these pages are warm, instructive, and perceptive. They illumine sacred lifeways that can have pronounced impact on our contemporary society and world. The wisdom shared throughout, while emanating from the ministerial life, translates to every vocation of compassion and care. There is a rhythm to this text, a musicality which flows from page to page, and a cadence not unlike the call and response of preaching that nourishes my own Black church tradition.

Reflecting the best of mentoring relationships, the scaffolding of this book wonderfully honors history, future, and vital practices of transformative exchange between two lives well and faithfully lived. The reader is engagingly drawn into this marvelous model of intergenerational witness and spiritual proclamation that is pivotal for the healing of disparate lives, divided lands, and anemic pulpits in our day and time. We cannot thank Karen and Morgan enough for sharing out of their faith and friendship. Their summons to joy is the music God hears. Thanks be to God!

ALTON B. POLLARD III
President and Professor of Religion and Culture
Louisville Presbyterian Theological Seminary

# Introduction

Morgan and I began our mentoring journey while I was as a student at Louisville Seminary and he was the Director of Field Education there. During my second and third years, we met each week to review sermons I prepared for my supply pastorate at a field education church. After we both departed Louisville, our mentoring relationship continued for all the rest of my years as a pastor of churches.

Ours has been a remarkable and life-changing journey that began when Morgan suggested I learn to preach without the presence of a manuscript. From there, our journey took us to many destinations in Scripture, theology, spirituality, and ministry experience. As you read and travel with us, ask yourself how mentoring could enrich your life or the lives of others. Our lives are all precious treasures of vast experiences; whether we are beginners or seasoned travelers. We can open those treasured lessons to others who are just beginning their journeys in ministry or other helping professions. Students and those new to their professions hunger for the wisdom of others who have faced the challenges they now face. A trusted mentor can provide encouragement and companionship throughout their ministries of service.

Morgan and I share our story because we want many more persons to put their toes into the water of this wonderful way of learning. We hope preachers, persons in the pew, and mentors from all disciplines will be encouraged in their journeys as they answer the call of God to give their lives in the service of others.

# CHAPTER ONE

# Prelude to a Journey

ONE WINTER AFTERNOON, I found myself on the campus of Louisville Seminary attending the funeral of my beloved uncle, Don. After his funeral, we buried his ashes behind the chapel with a marker saying, "Courage that perseveres." It had been more than twenty years since I had been in a church, but in that chapel, I felt something familiar. Something I hadn't felt for a long time.

After leaving the chapel the day of the funeral, I experienced some of the most turbulent years of my life. In 1997, I lost my job of eighteen years while working at a large suburban hospital. During my time there, I served as Administrative Director of Child and Adolescent Psychiatry and opened two psychiatric units and a therapeutic day school. Later, after receiving my MBA from Northwestern University, I served as Director of Quality Management, bringing the hospital the distinction of being named one of the top 100 hospitals in the United States.

When the hospital abruptly eliminated my job, I found myself lost in a sea of despair at the middle of what seemed like a successful career. The stirrings and rumblings of God's spirit, always present but generally hidden from my view, began to set in motion longings I had ignored in my pursuit of a successful career. I didn't listen right away. I still had my nose pointed to the ground, determined to fulfill my career aspirations. With those aspirations firmly in hand, I took a position of manager in the healthcare practice of Ernst & Young.

When I took that position, the partner who interviewed me commented that she wasn't sure I would fit into the culture of the firm. She observed that I had been a social worker and that my prior work was "helping people."

"That's not what we do here," she said.

But I was determined to fit in.

I didn't, but clients responded well to me, so I stuck with it. Then one night, I received some news that knocked me off my feet. I came back to the hotel after a long day at the client site. It was near midnight and I still hadn't picked up my voicemail. I rang up the firm's voicemail and was greeted with the words, "You have fifty-three unheard messages." I paced back and forth as I listened to the minutia of mail the firm had sent. Then came message seven. It was a nurse at the hospital in my hometown of Chester, Illinois.

"Your father has died," she said.

I collapsed on the floor, my head between my legs, sobbing.

The next day I left for Chester. When I drove into the small town of my youth, I walked into the funeral home, not knowing anything about what I needed to do. My parents were divorced, and my sister was estranged from Dad. I had never spoken to him about funeral arrangements. I was alone here, or so I thought.

As I walked into the funeral home, a woman from Dad's church (the church where I grew up) greeted me. She was a deacon. Joan stayed with me every step of the way. We navigated decisions about cremation, the memorial service, contacting family members, and obtaining the will. She was there for the funeral. Dad's funeral brought together family members who hadn't spoken with one another for years.

On the day of his funeral service, I walked down the narrow stairs of the church where I grew up to the church basement and saw long tables of pies, fruit, chicken, and potatoes. The church had prepared a meal for all of us. Finally, I felt like I was home. Before I left, I gave the deacon who had helped me Dad's car so she and her husband would have a reliable vehicle to drive while they did their deacon work. After that day, I was back to church for good.

I left Ernst & Young later that year to work for the Good Samaritan Society, a faith-based organization in Sioux Falls, South Dakota. While working there, I found myself surrounded by persons of faith who were putting their faith in action every day. Their work, which Lutherans refer to as vocation, was seamlessly woven into their faith. The word "vocation" comes from the word *vocare*, which means "to call." In that sacred place, the word "call" became an urgent and personal experience for me. It was the place where I began to sense a call to ministry.

Sense of call is what church people call this urgent need to follow wherever God leads. We don't presume to know that God called us. We only say we seem to sense that urging. My sense of call became so distracting that on one occasion I left my desk in the middle of the day, went back to my room in the central office building where I lived and fell on my knees in a tortured prayer where I finally said yes to God, but not without some fist shaking and a determined cry, "One day I will see you!"

Later that year, I was walking with my dear friend Cally on a forest preserve trail near my home in Chicago. In those days, I was a person who preferred to listen and enjoyed being with someone who could carry the conversation. Cally was a person who loved to talk. During a pause in our conversation, I gathered up my courage and said to her, "Cally, I believe God might be calling me to be a pastor."

We kept walking in silence for almost twenty minutes. Finally, I broke the silence.

"Do you have any reaction to this?"

After a few more moments she said, "I think it sounds right. Look at your life so far. You have always wanted to serve others. This step makes sense based on who you are and how you have lived your life so far."

Then I told her about a dream I had that week.

> I was climbing a high mountain. When I came to a precipice at the top, I looked out over the whole world. I was on top of the world, for a moment. As soon as I took in that glorious sight, I became blind. I felt my feet below me sliding on the rocks on that tiny perch at the top. I got

down on my hands and knees, determined to crawl my way down. Along the way I found a stick I used to test the patch of rocks ahead of me. Then, I heard a voice.

"I can help you get down."

I ignored it. But the voice continued and the sense of the presence of someone beside me was very strong.

"If you let me help you get down, we can go together. I can see the way. You won't be alone."

I clung to my stick for dear life.

"Take my hand," the voice said. "Let go of the stick and take my hand."

"Did you take the hand?" Cally asked.

"Yes, I did. And I heard that stick hit the rocks as it went down, down, down that mountain."

Cally's belief that I might be called to ministry was the only positive feedback I heard among those who knew me. To most everyone else, it looked like I had fallen off the cliff of a successful career. I was told I must be having a mid-life crisis. I needed to think this thing through.

A chaplain at the hospital where I had worked said, "Did you say you want to serve a church?"

He just shook his head in disbelief. What was I thinking? So many people believed my going into ministry was a mistake, I was tempted to forsake the whole thing. Cally's encouragement was part of what kept me in the game.

The pastor of my home church cautiously supported my sense of call. But she had some stern words.

"Don't go into ministry unless you find it is the only thing you can do in your life. Only go there when nothing else seems right." Then I told her I was spending a large portion of my days looking at seminary websites. She simply said, "Well, there you are."

Then came one last surprise. When I was packing the house to leave, I called my mother.

I put off that call until the last minute because I didn't believe she would approve of my decision to become a pastor. She was a Southern Baptist, and in her tradition, women could not become pastors. But Mom had a surprise of her own. She told me a story she had never told anyone.

When I was only a few months old, Mom attended a retreat with Dad. She left me home at the cottage with Dad and went to a church service on campus. In the service, the minister asked if anyone present would dedicate a child of theirs to mission work. Mom stood up. She never told anyone, not my Dad, a minister, a family member—no one! In those days, mission work was dangerous. Many missionaries didn't survive their journeys to foreign lands. Mom had waited for me for a long time. I was her first-born. She didn't know if she would have another child.

Her dedication that night was a huge risk. And a huge secret.

"Didn't you want to give up?" I asked her. I hadn't gone to church for almost twenty-five years. I will always remember her response.

"Sometimes these things take longer than we would wish."

Six years after the funeral in the chapel at Louisville Seminary, when I was fifty years old, I became a student there.

Ministry is a call. To all those folks who scratch their heads when a person with a successful career drops everything and goes into ministry, I offer my story. God calls people to do all sorts of things, not just ordained ministry. Have you had an experience where you called a friend and later that friend told you, "How did you know I needed so much to talk today?" God taps ordinary people on the shoulder every day, urging them to do something or say something no one else can do or say. Pastors aren't the only people who are called. We all are.

That sense of call was the reason I moved to Louisville in 2001. On the Sunday after my arrival in Louisville, I walked from my recently purchased house to the campus. Before going inside, I walked behind the chapel to see the marker of my uncle's grave and read again those words, "Courage that perseveres." Then I walked inside. Morgan saw me.

But I didn't see him. I was awash with all that had happened the week I left my home in Chicago. I had sat in the pew of my home church for the last time. In that service, we were invited to take a stone from a basket and hold it during the service. I took two more stones as I left the sanctuary, and I continue to keep them in the cupholder of my car. When I get behind the wheel, I sometimes glance at those stones or hold one in my hand before I put the car in gear.

As I walked into the chapel when Morgan saw me, I was thinking about the day before. The moving truck was scheduled to arrive at my house at 9 a.m. That same morning, I had a new piano delivered and the old piano taken away. Since the new piano didn't need to be moved all the way inside of the house, I left it outside on the sidewalk (no threat of rain that day). The moving truck was hours late. My good friend Margaret showed up to help while I was playing the piano on the sidewalk of my front yard. Neighbors gathered around me, even dogs stopped by to listen! By the time the moving truck arrived and was loaded, it was 4 p.m. and we were over five hours from Louisville. Because of these delays, the truck would not arrive in Louisville until after midnight and would not be unloaded until the following morning. When I set out for Louisville along with the moving van, I had to pack another bag so I would have food and clothing to bring with me to the empty house that awaited me.

That was one long drive. By the time I arrived in Louisville, it was dark. I could not read the print on the street signs in the neighborhood. It was midnight before I found the driveway of my new home. I shuffled through my glove box, finally finding a flashlight. Then I couldn't get the key to work in the realtor box. Finally, I was inside at last. I pulled my sleeping bag out of the car and curled up in the bag on the carpet in the basement of my new house, leaving on the light, just in case.

The next day I walked to the chapel. The moving van had unloaded everything that morning. I unpacked my travel bag, took a shower, and put on my travel clothes. Morgan noticed the hiking boots and day pack I had in tow the day I walked into the chapel. He told himself that day, "this one is a sojourner." I had a house full of boxes still unpacked. I literally didn't know where I was going, which was why I walked to the chapel that day instead of driving. I didn't want to get lost the next day, the first day of classes.

# CHAPTER TWO

# The Journey Begins

WHEN I WAS TWO months into seminary, my aunt, who knew many of the personalities at the seminary, said to me during dinner, "You must meet Morgan."

"Who is Morgan?" I asked. "Is he a professor or a PhD?"

My aunt just sighed and said, "You must meet Morgan."

I put it off. I couldn't imagine who this guy might be and why she thought I must meet him. Then one January morning, I slipped into the Field Education office of the seminary. After chatting with the office secretary for a while, I asked, "Is there a *Morgan* here?"

Her eyes brightened as she pointed to an open door. "He's right in there!"

I lingered quietly at the door, peeking inside and sizing up the situation. I thought I saw a bald head hiding behind a large computer screen. Then I got the courage to say his name, almost in a whisper. "Morgan?"

He popped up from his chair and came right to the door. He had wonderful bright eyes and a huge smile. Something about him reminded me of Yoda, the master jedi in *Star Wars*.

Morgan had a whimsical quality, and he seemed to enjoy listening more than talking. This was a trait I hadn't encountered very often as a seminary student.

Later that year, Morgan came to the first sermon I preached in front of people at my field education church. I worked and worked on that sermon. Polished up the words. Kept the stories simple and (I thought) compelling. I read the sermon with all the passion I could muster that day. Later, as we walked out to the car, Morgan said, "You could be a good preacher, but you must free yourself from the manuscript."

*Fat chance*, I thought. Never in a thousand years did I want, or think I would be able to do, such a thing.

"Let's have lunch," he said.

Lunch? I thought I would have to go home and sit alone at my desk, pondering the impossibility of preaching without notes. Instead, here were Morgan and his wife, Nora, asking if we could share a meal and talk about "regular things." That good meal helped me to swallow the mighty words he had spoken—"You must free yourself from the manuscript"—and created the possibility that those words might someday come true.

Later that summer, Morgan arranged for me to serve as a student pastor at a large church in Birmingham, Alabama. This was a church where Morgan had served as an interim pastor for three years. Before I left, Morgan pulled out the church directory to help me recognize some of the names and faces. I especially remember him pointing out a wonderful woman.

"Go talk to her," he said. "She will tell it like it is."

Part of my responsibilities there included preaching a weekly meditation at a nursing home. That is where I met the one who would "tell it like it is." Her name was Robbie Sevier. Robbie faithfully sat in one of those uncomfortable plastic chairs each Thursday, listening to me intently. Before I left, I sat down with her to have a conversation. She started out by telling me how much she had appreciated my preaching and how much she learned from my sermons. But then, quietly, she gently told me, "I wish you looked up from your manuscript. I wanted to see your face. I wanted to look into your eyes."

Wow! I had no idea anyone would want to see my face or look into my eyes. I was just a lowly student, trying to get through a very difficult seminary education. I spent hours of time grooming and touching up those one-page sermons. I left no word unturned, not a sentence untouched. I wanted the words to be right.

But here was a person who wanted to see my face. Look at my eyes. She wanted *that* more than she wanted all those carefully written words. She wanted to see who I was. Did I really believe what I was saying? Was there passion in my heart? Did I care about *her*, a lowly person in a nursing home who probably spent many lonely days in her room?

Yes, I did care about her. But did I care more about her than I cared about my precious words? Not so much. Robbie taught me two important lessons. The first was to love the people more than you love the production and final product that is called a sermon.

The other lesson was people want to look at your face, look into your eyes. They are searching for something, and you are right there, in front of them, sharing things about the God who loves them. They may not be sure about God's love, but they will figure out quickly what you love. And a look, a gesture, a graceful moment of eye contact, that is where they will find out the answer to questions like: Whom does she love? Does she really love God? Does she love me, too?

Those words stayed with me. As I journeyed home to Louisville from Birmingham, I tossed her words around in my mind, over and over.

When I arrived back on campus, I emailed Morgan about that first sermon he had heard and my experience in Birmingham

## MORGAN'S REPLY

"I was very glad I got to hear your first sermon, and that we had lunch together. Let me make it clear that I was not disappointed with your sermon. I can tell by meeting with you that you are a very perceptive student. In listening to the comment from the lady at the nursing facility who wanted to 'look into your eyes,' you've learned a very valuable lesson about preaching. Preaching can be one of the most pastoral and personal activities in which we engage—that is, it can be. Whether they analyze it or not, the people in the pew want something more than a fine sermon. They want to know if the preacher cares more about them than the sermon. This does not mean that we can do sloppy work with our sermons, but it does mean that we should ask ourselves as we prepare our sermons whether we want to touch the hearts of our people in a pastoral manner, or whether our real goal is to be seen, admired, and praised for having delivered an entertaining, interesting sermon. Another way to say this is that we've got to decide whether preaching is testimony or entertainment.

"Sadly, there's lots of entertainment going on in the pulpit. Maybe it has always been that way. If we've done a good job with our sermon and have been praised for our eloquence, it's tempting to enjoy the praise and want to continue doing well. After all, it's only natural to enjoy attention, and the attention we get, compared to what other professionals receive, is huge. Other professionals may receive much larger salaries, but how often do many of them get to enjoy having a large gathering of people listen to them, without interruption, for 20 minutes weekly? It can become very addictive, so much so that we come to enjoy the cultivation of our 'stained glass voice,' and all the praise and perks that go with it. And let's be honest in admitting that one of the perks is moving on to a larger, 'big steeple' church, where the weekly audience is larger—and the salary higher.

"If that happens to us, what we seldom notice is that, despite the eloquence of our weekly 'performance,' little nourishment has been given to hungry hearts. I can remember the instance of one such 'great preacher' who moved onward and upward to larger and larger pulpits. Producing great sermons left him with no time for pastoral work; he delegated that to his associate pastors. But when he finally retired, one of the quiet, little people of the congregation told me, with sadness, 'we really don't miss him because, after all, he never knew us.'

So, dear Karen, learning to preach without a manuscript is still a long way down the road for you. I just wanted you to start thinking about it as a goal. Preaching without a manuscript can make your preaching very effective. You will have constant eye-contact with your listeners, and it will be as though you are having a live conversation with them. That doesn't mean that it will be folksy, but it will have the power of an intimate contact with their hearts and minds.

"Added to this we must remember that preaching is one of the most personally revealing activities in which we engage. Sooner or later, our sermons reveal our hearts and what we love. That is why we need to remember that preaching is testimony, our weekly privilege of 'speaking a good word for Jesus.' As we write our sermons, and re-read them as we prepare for delivery, we must be asking ourselves, 'Does this really matter to me? Do I really intend to live by these words? Will my people hear some loving word for my Lord in this sermon?'

"Two of the pulpits in the churches I served were inscribed with written reminders, visible only to the preacher. One read, 'Sir, we would see Jesus,' (John 12:21 KJV). The other had a quotation from, I think, Richard Baxter, 'I preached as never sure to preach again, as a dying man to dying men.'[1] Both were sober reminders about the sacred task to which we have been called. We are not in the entertainment business! Karen, you are asking the right questions, the questions that a faithful shepherd asks. You're thinking about what is best for the sheep. Keep on listening!"

After receiving that email, I asked Morgan if he would help me with my weekly sermons at my pulpit supply church for the next two years of seminary. He said yes. But the words of his first email stayed with me for the many years of ministry that lay ahead.

## MY REFLECTIONS YEARS LATER

It has been many years since Morgan sent me those words. During all these years, I have struggled with the performance aspect of preaching. I react to criticism of my preaching with sulking episodes. Revising the words, over and over. Picking apart sermon tapes. Examining gestures.

I still want, more than anything, to be a better preacher. Although I can correct gestures, sentence structure, and flow of ideas,

---

1. Baxter, *Reformed Pastor*, 1620.

the biggest problem remains. I still want to be admired. I still put myself at the center.

A few years ago, I asked the persons attending services on Christmas Day to write on a piece of paper one thing they wanted to "fear not" the following year. The "fear nots" were collected and poured on a blue blanket like the blanket Linus carried in the *Peanuts* cartoon. We had watched a portion of the *Peanuts Christmas* movie. In that clip, Linus goes center stage and tells Charlie Brown what Christmas is all about. At one point, Linus drops his blanket. It is the only place in the *Peanuts* videos where Linus parts with his blanket, the place when he says, "And the angel said, 'Fear not . . .'"

We all gathered around the blanket and held it up like a flag is held over a coffin. I poured the pieces of paper that contained their "fear nots" on the blanket while I repeated the Scripture story in Luke again. When I read the words, "And the angel said, 'Fear not,'" we all dropped the blanket and those slips of paper. I rolled up the blanket with the papers in it and stashed it away in my office.

A month or so later, I had to move the blanket, and when I did, all the slips of paper fell out on the floor of my office. I saw that one of them had opened and I became curious. I took the papers home and read them. What fears do people bring to the sanctuary every Sunday? I was stunned. The comments included:

*Harm to the earth, loss, hate and gossip, illness, nuclear war, college and adulthood, people with opposing opinions in my personal life, depression and anxiety, despair, trouble breathing.*

I kept all those slips of paper in the room I use for study and prayer at home. Before praying, I look at one or two of them, remembering those who wrote them and asking God to help them fear not.

The people in the pews want something more than a fine sermon. They want to know the preacher cares about them and the things they carry in their hearts. When I looked long and hard at each one of those slips of paper, I realized their fears and needs were so much more important than my being admired! When people come to church, they are looking for a place where they can lay their burden down and listen for a whisper of good news. For years after coming home from services, I have collapsed in my chair, exhausted. Why? I didn't think standing in front and preaching for twenty minutes should wear me out.

But when I saw the contents of that blanket, I realized when I come home from a worship service, I am carrying in my heart the hardest questions people face. I am humbled to stand up and speak a word of good news during such basic, deep, human concerns. And I have found out I cannot do that unless I scrape around in the dark places of my own heart and face the darkness that dwells within me, too.

I worked for years in jobs where I was always wanting to move on up. Not anymore. This journey isn't up, it's down. Down to the places where we hide. The questions we dare not ask. The moments when all that really matters is whether I will care more about the people than the excellence of a sermon.

# CHAPTER THREE

# Solo Flight

IT HAS BEEN SAID speaking in public is one of the greatest fears human beings can face. A fear even greater than dying. I was often reminded of that fear when I preached funerals in my early years. In those days, the preacher was perched over an open casket. It was a bit like standing at the edge of a cliff, suspended between the person who had died and the people who were very much alive and waiting for me to speak to them. I tried to keep my eyes facing forward into the crowd, but occasionally I glimpsed the dead person lying at my feet. Then I would catch myself with a start and try to resume my public speaking with some semblance of dignity.

Morgan described the experience of preaching in front of people as "solo flight." In those early years, when I walked up front, the first thing I noticed was I was alone up there. If I dared to take a moment to gaze at the faces, I realized I wasn't only alone up there, but these people were waiting for me to say something. What, I wondered, would I say today? The only way to take off in this solo flight was to forget I was alone, forget all those people who were sitting there, and just start talking as if I were speaking to a trusted friend about the most important thing in the world. In Isaiah 40, we are told those who "wait on the Lord will renew their strength. They will mount up with wings like eagles. They will run and not be weary. They will walk and not faint" (Isa 40:31). Most Sundays, as

I walked to the front to preach, I would say in my heart one simple prayer, "O Lord, please help me to walk and not faint. O Lord, please help me to walk and not faint."

In my second year of seminary, before I preached my first Sunday as pulpit supply minister, Morgan and I laid out the ground rules of our work together. We would meet every week. I would bring a draft of the sermon I was working on and we would talk about it. We would also talk about how the prior week's solo flight had gone. Since Morgan wanted me to be three weeks ahead on my sermon writing, I had to write three sermons before my first Sunday of preaching in front of people.

"You need to get ahead on sermons," he said. "After all, what if some emergency demands pastoral attention and your sermon isn't written on Saturday night?"

The practice of being two to three weeks ahead on sermons served me well during all my years in ministry. Sermons that were already written sat on the back burner of my mind and were peppered and seasoned with the events that led up to the Sunday each one was delivered.

But I was still clinging to the manuscript.

"The development of a preacher is the work of a lifetime," Morgan said to me one day.

*Thank God for that*, I thought. *At this rate, a lifetime won't be long enough.*

I never actually read a sermon from a manuscript after my conversation with Robbie Sevier. Her kind and piercing words had made that impossible. Instead, I rolled up the manuscript in my right hand, walked down to the floor (on the level where the people were) and preached. Usually I forgot at least half of the sermon. When that happened, I just kept talking until I found my place in the manuscript. Looking back on those two years, I am eternally grateful people still sat there, listened as best they could, and shook my hand when it was all over. Preachers owe a huge debt to the people in the pews. A debt greater than they will ever know.

Each week, Morgan and I met. Each week I told him I could not let go of that manuscript. It would be like being cut off from the mother ship, left to drift in space. Of course, I was already drifting in space when I held the manuscript in my hand. But I still had that piece of paper I could open and read, which I felt was a much better option than running out of the sanctuary.

After hearing me tell him week after week that I was incapable of letting go of the manuscript, Morgan wrote down for me his thoughts about preaching without notes. His encouraging words helped me to imagine myself as a courageous preacher, able to look at the faces of the congregation and utter words from my heart.

## MORGAN'S REFLECTIONS ON PREACHING WITHOUT NOTES:

In my final year at Princeton Seminary, the senior homiletics course was taught by the dean of the faculty, Edwin Roberts. The goal of his class was to have all of us try to preach without dependence upon the manuscript. Two students would preach at every practice preaching class. The requirement was that we stand in the middle of the chancel behind a microphone (wireless microphones had not yet been invented) and deliver our sermon.

One of the books that we would read for the class was *Preaching Without Notes* by Clarence E. Macartney, the distinguished pastor of First Presbyterian Church of Pittsburgh. Macartney had recently retired but came to preach on one special evening in the seminary chapel. It was an unforgettable experience. Every pew in the chapel was filled as we watched this prince of the pulpit stand in the middle of the chancel (just as we had been required to do in our class, but without a microphone) and deliver a sermon entitled "Bring Up Samuel." I can still hear that sermon and its piercing conclusion. Macartney was a living example of his book's title.[1]

Dean Roberts realized that we might not choose to preach without notes when we arrived at our first church. I have no way of knowing whether the rest of my classmates thereafter tried to preach without dependence upon a manuscript, but for me the choice was simple:

1. Maccartney, *Preaching Without Notes*, 148.

I would never again preach from a manuscript for the remainder of my 41 years of ministry, as well as during my additional 6 years of interim ministry . . . and I still don't today upon those few occasions when I am invited to preach at a church.

So, why is freedom from a sermon manuscript so important? The answer lies in the definition of what a sermon is meant to be. A sermon should be a simple and loving conversation between the Christ in you (the preacher) and the Christ in them (the congregation). That being the case, a sermon is not something you do, but instead something that is done through you. Let's enlarge upon that definition.

The conversation between the Christ in you and the Christ in every other life is happening all the time, not just when you're standing in the pulpit. It is something that God, in Christ, is doing all the time as the Christ who is incarnate in every life is continually seeking recognition. This conversation does not depend upon our effort, but upon God's intention. This may not be apparent; many people appear to have no awareness of Christ's presence in the depths of their life. Still, in the most unlikely of lives, Christ is still present. As Paul Claudel once wrote, "In the heart of the meanest miser, the most squalid prostitute, the most miserable drunkard, there is an immortal soul with holy aspirations, which, deprived of daylight, worships in the night."[2] Although most of the human family may be unaware of Christ's deep and inner presence, Christ is still there. It does not depend upon their recognition, but upon God's intention to be present in every life. Whether they know it or not, everyone wants to find Jesus; He is the one for whom, beneath all their superficial desires, they're really seeking. Everyone is saying, "Sir, we wish to see Jesus" (John 10:21). We can become a part of their search for Jesus, and of God's search for them. What all of this means is that we need to "get out of the way" or, as we read in John 3:30, "He must increase, but I must decrease." Nothing must block this universal search for Jesus.

2. Predmore, "Poem," 104.

For starters, get your sermon manuscript out of the way. Have you ever noticed that as you read the story of Jesus in the gospels and hear him speaking to groups large or small, it is impossible to imagine him reading from a manuscript? The same is true of Paul as we hear him proclaiming his message on the Areopagus (Acts 17:22). You simply cannot picture Paul speaking from notes. As we reflect upon the preaching of either Jesus or Paul, we always see them, eye to eye, delivering their message from the heart. If we're tempted to reply that, after all, they were intellectual giants, it is clear, at least in the case of Jesus, that there is no suggestion in the gospels that Jesus received a formal education. He was a plain man of the people who functioned with the same mind as ours. And in the case of Peter and John as we hear them preaching in Acts 4:13, those that heard them "realized that they were uneducated and ordinary men." So, we have no excuse that allows us to be dependent upon our manuscript. Besides all that, as Canon Charles Raven once observed, if we're going to read "word for word" from a manuscript, why not have it printed and distributed to the congregation, allowing them time during the service to read it by themselves, after which we can respond to questions?[3]

It is also necessary to get our desire to perform out of the way. One of the perils of preaching without notes is that we will be tempted to enjoy our performance. When people see that you are preaching without dependence upon a manuscript, they will tell you how wonderful your preaching is in comparison to those other preachers who mostly read their sermons. This kind of praise will tempt you to make your sermons a performance, and you will begin to enhance your delivery with dramatic voice and body language, with a high-volume voice and big gestures. Your sermons will cease to be a simple and loving conversation. After all, many of us remember proposing marriage to a beloved life mate by looking into her eyes and saying, "I love you and want to spend the rest of my life with you." We didn't need a manuscript to

3. Raven, *Wanderer's Way*, 123.

make such a heartfelt proposal, nor did we resort to a big voice and dramatic gestures. When you learn to preach without notes, remember that preaching must never become a performance.

The flip side of this temptation to perform can be the fault of lapsing into sloppy conversation. Some preachers think that preaching without notes is the kind of delivery in which we "wing it." Preachers who make this mistake think it's O.K. to allow their delivery to be interrupted by the habits of casual conversation, pausing between sentences with an "uh" or "er" as though they are trying to form or remember their next sentence. Such shoddiness is not the aim of preaching without notes. Good preaching is the result of a carefully prepared manuscript which the preacher has studied and revised before entering the pulpit.

And then there's the pulpit itself as a temptation. Henry Ward Beecher is reputed to have said that the pulpit is an instrument of the devil because it comes between the preacher and the people. Even if he didn't say that, there's an important truth in those shocking words. It's rather amazing that, although we trace our origins from the man of Nazareth who never preached from a pulpit, we build sanctuaries with high and magnificent pulpits. Shadyside Church in Pittsburgh had such a high pulpit that I finally abandoned it, and delivered my sermons standing in the middle of the chancel, just as I had to do in my senior homiletics class. The high altitude of the pulpit can create a high attitude in a preacher. We can begin to think of ourselves as somehow higher than ordinary people, when the truth is that we are as ordinary as every other human being. The people who sit before us on a Sunday morning, as well as the people who never enter our sanctuaries are as close to Christ as we are. The cosmic Christ is pursuing every human life, and we are no exception to this loving quest. We are no holier or closer to Christ than anyone else on the face of the earth. Our prayers receive no more of God's attention than those of some wretched soul who cries for help from the gutters of human experience. We must never be deceived by the high altitude of our pulpit.

After about six months of preaching while holding my sermon rolled up in my right hand, I walked to the front empty-handed. I didn't feel free from the manuscript. But I noticed I could use my right hand while preaching. I'm not sure anyone in the congregation noticed. It wasn't the breakthrough I had anticipated. But it was a step. I continued to preach without a manuscript the following year.

As seminary was nearing an end, I wasn't sure what would happen next. I had put my resume online and had interviewed at a couple of churches, but two of the churches in which I was most interested had turned me down. In the Presbyterian denomination, a person cannot be ordained until a church calls them to be its pastor. Then my birthday rolled around. My classes were done, graduation was in two weeks, and I was treading water with no sign of employment in sight. Trying to keep my hopes up. Knowing nothing was certain. On the day of my birthday, Morgan called and asked if I would meet him at the student center. I sat down in one of those familiar chairs where Morgan and I had met to talk about sermons. Then I saw Morgan and Nora coming to the door. They had a birthday cake! I didn't even know Morgan knew it was my birthday. As we celebrated with students who passed through, I took a breath. I didn't know where I was going. I didn't know if I could even be a pastor. Yet, surrounded with all these unknowns, we celebrated. It was one of the kindest gifts I had received in a very long time.

Two months later, I had a call to a church in Indiana and Morgan moved to Florida. I called him and asked, "Can we continue our sermon conversations?"

He said yes.

# CHAPTER FOUR

# The Mentoring Room

WHEN MORGAN MOVED TO Florida and I moved to Indiana, we had to develop a different way of communicating with each other. Email correspondence became the way we connected and extended the mentoring experience from a face-to-face encounter to a distance-learning format. Because we had already been meeting face to face for two years, the email approach was an easy transition for us.

I wrote a sermon draft each week and sent it to Morgan. The sermon draft was for a sermon to be delivered three weeks later. This gave both of us plenty of time to iron out difficulties and make changes before the sermon was delivered. Then Morgan would send his reflections on the sermon a few days later. After receiving his feedback, I spent time (sometimes hours, sometimes days) letting his impressions sink in. Then I wrote a revised sermon and sent it to Morgan. He would comment again. We repeated that process until both of us were comfortable with the final product. During the many years we corresponded that way, I would wait each week for his response, looking for his email each time I opened my computer. Just knowing there was someone on the other end, someone reading my sermon, was a tremendous support to me. In my waiting, I was always wondering what he would say. After many years of working together, I eventually became able to predict his comments and make changes before I sent the sermon to him.

Behind the scenes of these email conversations, something else was taking place. We were both creating a "mentoring room." The mentoring room was the place we entered when we had these conversations. Present in the mentoring room were Morgan and I, the Holy Spirit, the sermon draft, and the Scripture. In that room, anything could happen. The creative process continued in the mentoring room of our minds and hearts. Whole sermons might be abandoned. Personal reflections might be changed. Interpretations of Scripture might be tossed about. The context of the congregation would be considered. The secret to our making full use of the mentoring room was our trust in each other, in God, and in the process. We both had to let go of what we wanted to happen and allow what needed to happen, to happen. Morgan described this in a previous chapter as: "The conversation between the Christ in you and the Christ in every other life is happening all the time, not just when you're standing in the pulpit. It is something that God, in Christ, is doing all the time as the Christ who is incarnate in every life is continually seeking recognition. This conversation does not depend upon our effort, but upon God's intention."[1]

In her book, *The Third Room of Preaching*, Marianne Gaarden says listening to preaching produces a similar dialogue.[2] Preaching is not a monologue where the preacher simply speaks, and the congregation simply listens. The outer voice of the preacher is only one of many voices within the listener, whose mind is not silent, but in a world filled with thoughts.

The preacher is a dialogue partner and facilitator who enables the listener to create their own insights. In the process, the listener may forget the specifics of the sermon itself and create their own inner sermon based on their own life experiences. They enter a third room much like the mentoring room Morgan and I experienced. While the words of the sermon are being spoken, the listeners weave those words into a tapestry of their own creation, creating

---

1. These words are found in "Morgan's Reflections on Preaching without Notes," in chapter 3.

2. Gaarden, *Third Room of Preaching*, loc. 1091 of 3461.

meaning for their lives. In the words of Gaarden, "there are as many sermons as there are listeners."[3]

In our mentoring experience, Morgan and I retreated to such a room where we brought our knowledge and life experiences. Each week we both listened to the words of the sermon I would preach. We each responded to those words in the context of our own lives. We both encountered the guidance of the Holy Spirit speaking through the words of Scripture, the words we shared with each other, and the words of the sermon. Through this process, new meanings sprang up. All those meanings were written down in emails, culled in both of our minds and hearts, and shared with each other. We did this for over fifteen years. In that time, we were able to be in each other's minds as we entered the mentoring room. It was a unique and precious experience for both of us. Gaarden describes such experiences as an act of divine grace. An act of participating in Christ. Our conversations in the mentoring room enabled me to speak of God out of the shared humanity I experienced with Morgan in the mentoring room. Karl Barth described this speaking of God as, "Ministers ought to speak of God. We are human, however, and so cannot speak of God. We ought therefore to recognize both our obligation and our inability and by that very recognition give God the glory."[4]

## DEAR READER, JOIN US IN THE MENTORING ROOM!

Early in 2006, Morgan and I had a mentoring conversation about the story of the massacre of the innocent children after Jesus' birth that is described in Matthew 2. I began the conversation with a question and a sermon draft. My question was, "Why does Matthew tell a story about the slaughter of innocent children where only the Christ child is saved? What about all those other children? Couldn't they have been saved, too? I also sent him a sermon that was full of problems. Here are some excerpts from that problem sermon, titled "Back to Normal."

3. Gaarden, *Third Room of Preaching*, loc. 1461 of 3461.
4. Barth, *Word of God and the Word of Man,* 109.

## SERMON: BACK TO NORMAL

**(full text can be found in: https://mentoringwithmorgan.com/resources/)**

Christmas is coming to an end. Back to normal. Time to drag the tree out to the curb, put away the decorations, finish up all those holiday goodies and settle in for a long winter's nap. One thing I love to do after the stress of holiday celebrations is to come home. Settle back down in my house and routine. Get back to normal. I am guessing that is what Mary and Joseph wanted to do, too. They had made a long journey to Bethlehem and Mary had given birth. We do not know the details, but I suspect they were glad to get back home after that eventful night of shepherds, angels, and birth in such a cold place.

Back to normal. Well . . . maybe not. Our story in Matthew today does not paint a picture of returning to the quiet life. In that story, Joseph had a dream. An angel told him to "Get up! Flee! Herod wants to kill your son!"

So, Joseph, Mary and Jesus fled to Egypt. They were refugees. While they were hiding in Egypt, Herod had all the male babies in Jerusalem who lived in or around Bethlehem killed.

Morgan responded to my first sermon with this reply:

One of the big problems with any sermon upon this text is that Matthew 2 is an extremely difficult passage upon which to preach a sermon. My guess is that all too many sermons have been written upon the passage without due regard to the problems within the text. Even after those problems are faced, the larger problem is how to deal with them in a sermon.

Problem #1 is the fact that the Matthew story simply cannot be harmonized with Luke's nativity story, which, it seems, you have decided to try (!) However, if we take Matthew 2 as it stands, there are no shepherds and angels, and no birth in a manger. After all these events in Luke, the holy family returns "to their own town of Nazareth." But in Matthew, they never get there until after their time as refugees in Egypt. Then Joseph "made his home in a town called Nazareth." Not in Bethlehem. So, we don't really have a way of solving the conflict between these stories, and my approach has always been to acknowledge this fact "up front" as an inexplicable conflict. Then we can set the mood for dealing with the other conflicts that occur in the story.

Thus, we ask the congregation to put away the standard nativity scene images of the Christmas story and travel with us to Bethlehem where, for some unexplained reason, it is assumed that they are living in a "house."

Problem #2 is that much of the story is unbelievable, especially the wandering star which somehow "stopped" over the very street address where the holy family lives. I realize that you have tried to explain why "all Jerusalem" is frightened; however, the story seems rather to be painted with the large brushstrokes of a fairy tale, which is what I take it to be. Or better yet, as a Jewish Haggadah, an elaborative story created upon the basis of various texts. You might not want to get into these technicalities. But it's O.K. to acknowledge the difficulties.

Problem #3 is that Matthew passes over the massacre of the infants almost as though it doesn't matter to him. For him, it is an interesting fulfillment of prophecy, like the rest of his story, throughout which he is telling us that all kinds of prophecies are being fulfilled. So, my inclination, if I were writing a new sermon upon this passage, would be to say, "Hold it, Matthew, there's a big hole right in the middle of your story that demands some reflection. If God was so interested in warning and guiding Joseph for the sake of the Christ child, why does your God seem so indifferent to the slaughter of so many innocent children? Why doesn't God warn those parents of what was about to happen to their children?"

So, my approach would be to call attention to this painfully unanswered question that remains awkwardly right in the very middle of Matthew's account and to move from there to the same unexplained horror stories that continue to be present right in the middle of every Christmas season.

One of the most meaningful holiday seasons of my ministry was spent preaching in the First

Presbyterian Church in Nashville in December 2000. I had been brought in as an "interim" because of a ministerial crisis. Every weekend, we were housed in a small apartment, next to another apartment in which a family that had survived the massacre in Rwanda was staying. Along with the parents there were five children of varying ages. The rest of their family had been slaughtered. The walls between our apartments were thin, so we could hear the family singing the songs of Christmas in preparation for participation in the worship services every week. I don't know how they were able to continue singing under such circumstances. Their joy amidst darkness and death made the music of our TV Christmas specials, plus all the canned music in our retail stores seem like a profane mockery of the real music of Christmas. As I heard them singing, I remembered reading how so many more people had been brutally hacked to death in Rwanda than those who had died in our World Trade Center. The tragedy, however, is that probably 98% of American citizens can't even find Rwanda on a world map.

How can we keep on singing while the massacre of the innocents continues? The massacre of the innocents in Matthew 2 never made it into the headlines; such news had to travel by word of mouth. But we know that when such things happen, we are not powerless. We can do something about such needless deaths, whether they occur because of wicked leaders (as in Darfur) or because of war (as in Iraq), or because of grinding poverty and disease.

I have the feeling that, in your writing of this sermon, an idea embedded in the title has been forced upon the passage. My guess is that this would be a tighter sermon if you could confine your thrust to weeping and active waiting. The text confronts us with what is always a horrible reality during our glib Christmas celebrations. Matthew passes over it all too quickly, and we seem to hasten on with him, so here is a chance to listen to Rachel's weeping and decide what we ought to be doing about it as we await God's coming in judgment. Your paragraph on Rachel's weeping is the only time in any sermon I've ever heard when a preacher has taken time to pay attention to the

plight of Rachel and her children, so there's the direction
that you can take. It will make Matthew 2 come alive in a
new and urgently important way. I hope this offers some
direction for making this a simpler and more direct sermon upon the suffering heart of this story.

After I read this feedback, I sent a revised sermon back to
Morgan. Here is the revised sermon titled, "Rachel Weeping."

## SERMON: RACHEL WEEPING (MATT 2:12–21)

I usually breathe a sigh of relief after Christmas Day. The
rush is over, and the new year has not yet begun. These
days are meant to be quiet. Restful. Perhaps the most
restful part of these days after the holidays is the experience of returning home. Persons who are visiting me
return to their homes, which makes my world a quieter
place . . . or I return to my home from visiting family and
have that sense of relief when I walk in the front door.
Maybe more than anything else in the world, I love to
come home.

The story we will hear today is a disturbing one. It
is a story that disrupts that peace on earth I seek so dili-
gently after the holidays. It is a story about leaving home.
A story about grief and weeping. A story that reminds
us that the world where Jesus was born is not so very
different from our own.

The story we hear today should be difficult for any
serious Christian because the problem of human pain and
suffering still faces us at its stark and terrible maximum.
"Why didn't God protect those other babies?" Matthew
doesn't even ask that question; instead he passes over the
massacre of the infants almost as though it doesn't matter to him. In fact, this incident is not even mentioned in
the historical documents of the time. One must assume
that the murder of a few baby boys in a small town wasn't
an item that warranted serious report.

But then, we hear something. It is something that is
quiet at first, coming from far away. Listen. Can you hear

it? It is the sound of weeping. Matthew tells us that this weeping is coming from the grave of Rachel, the mother of all Israel. This is how Matthew reports it: "Thus says the LORD: 'A voice is heard in Ramah, lamentation and bitter weeping. Rachel is weeping for her children; she refuses to be comforted for her children, because they are no more.'"

Rachel wept. The image is from the book of Jeremiah and it takes place in Ramah. The exiles were leaving their homes to travel to Babylon. As they began that long journey, about five miles out of Jerusalem, they passed Rachel's grave. As the exiles walked away from the ruin of Jerusalem, the wreckage of the temple, and everything they knew as home, they could hear Rachel, the mother of Israel . . . weeping. Weeping, even in her grave. Weeping, for her children who were "no more." Ramah is an image of our world, and the cry we hear is the voice of our world's weeping. Matthew pauses, for just a moment, to show us this image as he tells us that Jesus was homeless, too. Jesus was sent away from his home to Egypt to escape the murder of those innocent babies.

Isn't this a little like our world? As we deck our halls, sing our carols, and watch our Christmas TV specials, horrible events are taking place. More than 2.5 million people have been driven from their homes in Rwanda. As many as 400,000 people have died in the genocide there, and the UN officials estimate that the death toll in Rwanda could rise catastrophically if the perilous humanitarian situation falters. Up to 100,000 people could die each month.

During the dying, can you hear something? It is something that is quiet first, coming from far away. Listen. Can you hear it? It is the sound of weeping. How can we keep on singing and praising God when massacres of innocent children continue? I don't know. But I do know that when such things happen, we are not powerless. We can do something about such needless deaths whether they occur because of wicked leaders or because of war, or because of grinding poverty and disease. We can do something, and doing something is, after all, how Christians ought to be celebrating the coming of the Prince of Peace and the realization of God's reign on earth.

And maybe the place to start is by weeping. It's hard to imagine weeping to be an act of strength . . . even a political act . . . but it is. When we weep, we are saying, "These children matter! I care about these people! They have a place in the world, and they are gone! I will not allow their departure to go unnoticed!" Jesus wept at the grave of a friend before he died. He cared enough to weep. Mary wept at Jesus' grave on Easter morning. And Rachel wept for the exiles that were sent far from their homes, not knowing if they would ever return.

But listen, do you hear it? It is another sound. The sound of a voice speaking to Rachel as she weeps. Do you hear it? It is the sound of the Lord! The Lord says, "The days are surely coming, says the Lord, where I will make a new covenant . . . I will put my law within them, and I will write it on their hearts . . . no longer shall they teach one another or say to each other, 'Know the Lord' for they shall all know me, from the least of them to the greatest, for I will forgive their iniquity and remember their sins no more." (Jeremiah 31)

Going home. They are going home. The exiles will return home. Jesus will return to a new home in Nazareth. The children of Israel will be brought home. You see, right in the middle of the killing, the hate, the despair . . . is our Savior. It's a message easy to miss. It's a message that speaks in whispers, in silence. The war, the hate, the suffering . . . these are easy to hear, easy to read about. We are a people who get our daily fix of bad news from the newspaper, the television, and the internet. We are a people accustomed to hearing the noise of bad news as our daily bread.

But I want to leave you today with a gentle glimpse of the good news. Jesus has come. Jesus has come to us, where we live. Right here, in the middle of our sinful, messy lives. Jesus has come, and Jesus is still alive. In the meantime, we are not a people who must weep without hope. We are a people who are going to be brought home.

A friend of mine called me a couple of weeks ago to tell me that her mother, who has been suffering greatly these past few months, was near death. As she talked, we wept together. I have known Peg since seminary, and Peg has cared for her mother for many years. Peg told me that night she knew her mom was near death when they took her to the hospital and her mother said, "What are all these other people doing here?" Peg asked.

"What other people?"

Then Peg's mom told of relatives and friends that had died years ago. She was seeing her departed loved ones. A homecoming was being prepared for her. She was being brought home, and a celebration was being planned.

In these quiet days after Christmas, before the new year begins, listen to the quiet truth of redemption, that whisper of hope that rose up during bloody Bethlehem. It comes to us again this year. "For God so loved the world . . ."

Amen.

Oh, how tempting it was for me to harmonize something that just wouldn't neatly snap together, like pieces of a puzzle. I was out of seminary four years before Morgan helped me to discover the Christmas stories in Matthew and Luke could not be fitted together into an orderly nativity scene. The fact Matthew reports this horrifying story of babies killed in Bethlehem without a pause reminds me of the world I have lived in during all these years of ministry. Perhaps it has always been this way.

Many years after Morgan sent me his thoughtful response about Bethlehem, I had to preach an Advent sermon three days after the killing of children in Sandy Hook School. However, for some inexplicable reason, I didn't change course. I told myself the sermon I had already prepared for that Sunday would be fine. I pulled it out and I preached it. Oh, how foolish and arrogant I was, to act like Friday didn't happen, believing I could deliver a sermon that failed to mention and deal with such a horrific event on the following Sunday morning!

After services, one of my thoughtful parishioners stopped me and said, somewhat apologetically, that after Sandy Hook, she wanted to hear some words of comfort, some words that reflected that a horrible event that had happened only three days earlier. I wept when I got home. I also sent an email to Morgan, asking for some advice (and probably comfort).

Morgan sent me a reply that was totally anticipated. "Don't preach words of comfort! Challenge the congregation to ask serious questions about why these children died! What events in our world made such a terrible event possible? What should a disciple of Christ be doing now, in the wake of this horror?"

My head was spinning. I preached a sermon that ignored Sandy Hook, almost the same way Matthew passed over the murder of the innocents with no comment at all. My parishioner wanted to be comforted, and my mentor told me I should be challenging the congregation to wake up and ask ourselves, "What does God call us to do in such a world?"

From conversations in the mentoring room came lessons, precious lessons. Don't cut and paste the Scriptures to make one story out of Matthew and Luke. Don't ignore horrible events. Include them in weekly sermons. Don't let those horrible events disappear in the ether of another day of numbed-out denial. And don't comfort when a bracing "Why?" is necessary.

While teaching a confirmation class during the Pulse shooting disaster in Orlando, I asked that class of fifteen-year-olds who were born in 2001 how they responded. They shook their heads.

"It just happens all the time. I try not to think about it."

That is our greatest temptation: to try not to think about it. But we still live in a bloody Bethlehem world. The pain is so great, we have even stopped crying. Perhaps we too, like Rachel, need to cry and cry and cry for our children who are on their way to being "no more." Some of these questions just go on and on. But the crying, it should never stop, and the "doing something about it" that follows should always continue. After all, we have the promises of God that go with us.

"For God so loved the world."

## CHAPTER FIVE

# Early Lessons 1: In Times of Trouble

THE SERMON EXAMPLE OF Rachel weeping came during my early years of serving as a pastor. During those beginning years, I had so much to learn. The first few years when someone called me pastor I had to pause. Were they talking to me? Although members of my congregation knew me only as a pastor, I had known myself for fifty years as something else. Being a pastor took some getting used to.

Along with this new role and new title came new problems. Most of these problems came in the form of unvoiced expectations. Although mind-reading wasn't one of the skills I learned in seminary, many persons seemed to believe I already knew what they needed, expected, or wanted. Was this information supposed to be revealed to me by God now that I was a pastor? Many times, I even wondered if, as a pastor, I should be able to figure these things out.

The most challenging times were times of conflict. Being the target of painful conflict is especially difficult because a minister can't discuss her problems *in* the congregation with any member *of* the congregation. Even the beloved spouse of a pastor can become perplexed and frustrated with the congregational conflicts his wife faces.

What does this have to do with sermon writing? Plenty.

The one place where a minister can speak uninterrupted, with no need to defend herself, is in a sermon. The temptation to preach at one's enemies can be almost overwhelming. Even when I would try to take every precaution when writing sermons, stuff would slip in.

In April 2008, Morgan sent me an email about one such sermon. He began with these words: "My overall reaction to *Kept in Unity* (in its present form) is that it will make trouble for you, unless you remove from it all references to your church situation." Trouble would be an understatement. In that sermon I opened with a story about Peter Gomes, the distinguished Harvard preacher. Peter's mother was nearing her death, and she was concerned there would be people in heaven she didn't get along with on earth. Peter tried to reason with her, telling her the presence of Jesus would dissolve any such problems. But his mother was having none of it. After that story and the reading from John 17, I opened the sermon with these words: "Most sermons don't begin with a warning, but today I feel we need one. This is not an easy topic for a sermon. It is not an easy topic for those who hear the sermon. Jesus asked, and he asked again, that we have unity. Yet, how scarce it seems to be. Where there is competition, divisions, exclusiveness, or bitter dissention, the cause of Christianity is harmed, and the prayer of Jesus is frustrated. The gospel cannot truly be preached in any congregation of Jesus Christ when these things are present."

## *MORGAN'S RESPONSE*

Your scripture introduction is fine; after that, however, don't begin with a warning. From the outset, this will create anxiety about what's coming in the sermon. Such a sentence as, "The gospel cannot truly be preached in any congregation when competition, divisions, exclusiveness or bitter dissention are present," should be dropped. After all, it's not true because there is no congregation in which some disunity is not present. On the second page, drop such references as, "Is there any one in our church that you have recently had a misunderstanding with?" What I am saying is that you must talk about this disunity in a way that is not accusatory or anxiety-producing. You don't want any listener to be thinking, "I wonder who

Karen is talking about?" So, my advice is to "lighten up" this sermon so that we can make it heavier as we carry them along with us. We don't want to lose them in the beginning, so let's start with something light and maybe even humorous. Right after your scripture introduction, try this story that just happened this morning.

"An old friend of mine spends three mornings every week tutoring Hispanic migrant farmworker children. The parents of most of these children are in their 30s and their grandparents whom they seldom see (and who are in their 50s) are mostly in Mexico. Thus, my friend is the age of their great grandparents whom they have never seen. As the children were lining up for lunch, one of them said to my friend, "You're very old, aren't you?" He admitted that he was very old. Another child then asked, "How old are you?" My friend told them that he was 80 years old. A third child then said, "Then you're so old that you're going to die!"

Well, there does come a time in our life when we know that most of our life is behind us, and that death cannot be all that far away. Like Peter Gomes' mother, our inward thoughts turn more and more to heaven and what it will be like. When this happens, we must surely realize that there are people with whom we haven't gotten along with on earth who will probably be there also. We may have been estranged from them for many years. Maybe it was someone with whom we worked. Maybe we were their boss and had to fire them. Or maybe it was a neighbor, or even a member of our family. Maybe it was the husband or wife from whom we were divorced. What will it be like to be in the same heaven with them? How will heaven ever be heavenly if we must find a way to live with the very people with whom it was impossible for us to live on earth? When such questions arise in your mind (and they will sooner or later), how will we deal with them? I'm hoping that we don't dismiss these questions by hoping that such former enemies won't make it into heaven. After all, we'd better not count upon such an easy out. Or do we get around the problem by hoping that heaven is like a huge city, maybe New York or Los Angeles, so that we won't run into those difficult people very often? But my guess is that we'd better not rely upon that solution, even though heaven will have to be large enough to contain all the children of God through all the ages.

"Maybe we'd better think in terms of the 'worst case scenario' in which we find that our place in the great heavenly chorus is right next to that very person whom we just couldn't stand to be near on earth. What will we do then, if we discover that we didn't get the special seating for which we had hoped?

"At this point, you will have created a stage upon which people can reflect upon their disunity with some difficult person in their life. As you get to the end, I like your story about the CEO sitting next to his cleaning lady in heaven. Suggest that they think through an average day, looking at various people in their lives and wondering, 'Is this the one with whom I'll be sitting in heaven?' Think about the nameless man who picks up your garbage. The Latino lady who cleans your office. Your troublesome neighbor. Or maybe even some member of this church who is sitting right in this sanctuary this morning. (You see how we save this one for last).

The day I read those words, I felt like I had been rescued from a raging river. I stepped back. I recognized how my hurt and anger were presenting themselves in the words of a sermon. I find humility is a scarce commodity when I am in the vortex of conflict. But the day I received these words from Morgan, I tasted the sweet nectar of God's grace. I gave thanks to God for Morgan. I rested in the truth of his words and gave myself a break. Perfection was taken off the menu that day.

This single email didn't put an end to the church conflicts I was facing. It didn't rescue me from ever-mounting efforts to make myself look good, or to try—yet again—to please everybody. It didn't even teach me the humility I was so desperately seeking. One email or a single conversation cannot do that.

But a single conversation could lift me up that day, put me on more stable ground, and restore my hope to someday be a good pastor. All those moments, emails, and the laughs and the sorrows in the words we shared helped me to just go on. When no solutions were in sight, no hints for better times brightened the darkness, these conversations sustained me for one more step, one more day, and eventually for many years to come. In the meantime, while the healing and the learning went on behind the scenes, I could grab a restful night and awake refreshed for the new tomorrow ahead of me.

CHAPTER SIX

# Early Lessons 2: Love is Patient

EARLY IN JANUARY 2010, I decided to write a sermon on 1 Corinthians 13. Before I even started, I knew I had wandered into some very challenging terrain. I sent an email to Morgan saying, "I approach this chapter with fear and trembling. These are such lofty words about love. What more could anyone say? Yet . . . I have added a few of my own thoughts." Here is a sample of some of those thoughts.

### SERMON: A STILL MORE EXCELLENT WAY

Although Paul talks of love with lofty grandeur, most of what he had to say to his churches was less than warm and cozy. The letter to Corinth, where these words of love are found, was riddled with warnings and rebukes. Corinthians were described by writers of the day as persons without grace or charm. The wealthy people were coarse and objectionable. The poor had to grovel for the smallest morsels of food. In this one letter alone, Paul addressed circumstances where the poor were being excluded from participation in the Lord's Supper, incidents of sexual immorality had occurred, and competition over who had the most impressive spiritual gifts continued.

The question of who had the most impressive spiritual gifts was the issue that gave rise to 1 Corinthians

13. Members who were able to "speak in tongues" felt superior to those who could not. This conflict was the grain of sand that served as the irritant that created one of the most beautiful passages of Scripture ever written. Such is the nature of God's work in our lives. In our most exasperating struggles, we find the seed of something new and wonderful.

What is love? Let's look at one of the adjectives Paul used to describe love. Love is patient. During Abraham Lincoln's political life, no one treated him with more contempt than William Stanton. Stanton called Lincoln a "low cunning clown." He nicknamed Lincoln "the original gorilla" and said that scientists were a fool to wander about Africa trying to capture a gorilla when they could have found one so easily in Springfield, Illinois. Lincoln did not rise to the bait. He made Stanton his war minister because Stanton was the best man for the job. He treated Stanton with courtesy. The years wore on. The night came when the assassin's bullet murdered Lincoln. In the little room where President's body was taken stood Stanton, looking down at Lincoln's face. He said through his tears, "There lies the greatest ruler of men the world has ever seen." The patience of Lincoln had the last word. His love won the day, even in his death.

Our culture is so impatient, we usually think of patience as a lack of impatience! Such a view can cause us to believe patience is passive. Not so. Waiting patiently is not like waiting in line at the drugstore, waiting for the rain to stop, or waiting for the sun to rise. The word patience comes from the Latin verb *patior,* which means "to suffer." Our impatience is an indication that, somewhere down there in the depths of our heart is the acid of unkindness that needs the healing medicine of Jesus' presence. We have this very chapter in Corinthians because the patience of an apostle was being tested by a bickering people.

Patient love works its miracles quietly. It's whisper echoes through the ages. These are the things that are remembered. These are the things that are eternal. Lincoln didn't live to see the outcome of his loving actions toward Stanton. Yet, those very actions are still remembered today, even as we reflect on them here. How would our lives be different if we remembered that our expressions of patient love to each other were the only things that would survive after our life was done? Such love changes lives, and changes life itself.

## *MORGAN'S RESPONSE*

I've come across some thoughts on impatience in rereading Henry Drummond's *The Greatest Thing in the World.*[1] If you don't have a copy of that little classic, it's one you should "sell your bed and buy" because it's still as powerful an exposition of 1 Corinthians 13 as was ever written. My own copy from the early 20th century is almost falling apart from age and constant rereading. I read it today when I lost my temper in dealing with a technical service agent in trying to solve a printer problem. True, this agent had badly botched the job he was supposed to be doing (and for which I had paid a decent amount of money in purchasing their support contract). He was so incompetent that, not only did he fail to solve the problem, he also rendered our two other computers without printing connections. Still, it bothered me greatly that I lost my temper and hung up on him. I didn't call him any names or that kind of thing; it is just that I was angry . . . and my useless anger didn't solve anything.

Reading Drummond's words has reminded me of the eternal urgency of dealing with an impatient, ill-tempered spirit in myself. Ill temper can be the one blot on an otherwise noble character (not that I'm noble). But it is a serious blot because, as some rash or unkind word suddenly erupts, it is the surface symptom of something that has come from some place in the depths of my being where I need conversion and healing. There is an urgency in dealing with our impatience and cultivating, instead, a patient spirit, because the moments in time when we

---

1. Drummond, *Greatest Thing in the World.*

touch eternity are those few times in our lives when we can be lovingly patient.

I responded to Morgan the next day with these words:

I was very moved by your email today. In fact, I enjoyed your words even more than the words of Drummond! The experience of losing my temper when things don't go my way is one of the most unsettling experiences I have. But when I encounter those times, I can sense the gentle wind of grace washing over those places in my heart. I guess that for all the years I live, there will be places in my life God's grace hasn't yet reached. Someday, that will not be so. In the meantime, I muddle along and do my best to trust God.

Later that day, Morgan sent me one final response:

Maybe it's crazy, but I think God forgave me for my ill-temper by allowing me to get all three computers connected to the replacement printer . . . and all by myself without any technical support. All day long I worked at being patient, so now I can rest for the night without any regrets.

A decade passed before I realized how the context surrounding this sermon had formed its content. That context is described by an email I sent Morgan after receiving his message of the story of losing his temper on the phone:

It's been a tough week. Our office manager has been in the hospital all week. When I visit her in the hospital, I can see that she is losing ground in her battle with cancer. Then I got an intestinal virus that had me up all night. I haven't been this sick in many years. I got a call from hospice yesterday, and mom isn't eating much. She sleeps most of the time, and she has lost 7 lbs. this month. Dan has been a wonderful help and support. We are moving along in our wedding plans.

Morgan replied to this email with the following words:

> With your background as a therapist, you've probably guessed that your physical illness may have been caused by the stress of being overworked. You've got lots of stuff on your plate (your Mom and your forthcoming marriage, and all your pastoral work). Don't let this all interfere with your wedding plans. You deserve your dreams.

I was living in the valley of the shadow of death, struggling with wedding plans and the decision to marry Dan after being single for over thirty years, and trying to write a sermon about love! I was both thrilled and apprehensive about my wedding plans, worried whether my love for Dan was deep and sturdy and strong enough for us to take this momentous step. This was the act on center stage of my life, while in the background were images of my office manager dying of cancer and my mother dying in hospice. Trying to keep my footing in this whirlwind of events, what could I say about love?

Love is patient. It's tough. It works its miracles quietly. Patient love is the character of God, and when we show that love to one another, we are participating in the very life of God. Ten sometimes patient years later, I am now enjoying a marriage that began late in life. I am beginning to embrace my dreams and allow myself to deserve them. I am learning to love the persons who have always loved me.

And what about loving my enemies? There was a time I thought I didn't have any enemies. I didn't understand all those references in the psalms to one's enemies. Who were these people? The Russians? The terrorists? Some pesky technician who doesn't know how to fix a computer? After five decades of living, I realized my enemies were persons who I felt opposed me, persons I chose to view as my enemies. In ministry, I found more than enough of these enemies to justify all the attention paid to them in Psalms. Many of these enemies were within me, not outside of me. Others were part of my daily life in ministry. How could I even begin to love these people? I even told my mother once, "I know Jesus loves everybody, and we are supposed to love our enemies, but I just can't."

It was then that a friend asked me if I ever prayed for my enemies. I was startled into silence. When I went home and tried to do it, I couldn't. I was too mad to pray for them. But the Holy Spirit kept watch as I tried again and again until finally, I could utter a sincere word of prayer for a person I couldn't be in the same room with. Morgan had helped me get started on that journey the day he told me the story of the technician who instead of fixing a printer, broke all three printer connections. A story for which I am forever grateful.

## CHAPTER SEVEN

# Later Lessons: Telling it Like it is

PLAYING IT SAFE IS a big temptation that has lured many preachers (and congregations) into toned-down, easy-to-swallow sermons. I was one of those preachers. I recognized the gospel was about the most radical thing I had ever read, but on Sunday morning it didn't always sound that way. One year, when the congregation would focus on the gospel of Luke, I preached a sermon about Jesus' first sermon in the synagogue of his hometown. Jesus had some stirring words to share that day.

### *SERMON: WELCOME TO LUKE (PORTIONS)*

I remember the first sermon I preached here in Elgin. Pastors call that sermon a "candidating" sermon because the minister is preaching as a candidate to a church. After the sermon, the church would dismiss the candidate from the sanctuary and vote on whether they would call her to be its pastor. First sermons, like first impressions, are important. In seminary, I was instructed to "steer clear" of controversial issues in the "candidating" sermon. That first sermon is generally not the time to launch into a theological quagmire of questions that the best pastors still puzzle over. Not the time to start a campaign about the political issue of the day. First sermons

43

generally take place on safe territory. They say something about the preacher, but not anything too difficult for the congregation to hear. After all, there are hundreds of sermons later (that is, if the preacher gets a positive congregational vote) to dip into the places where angels, and pastors, fear to tread.

Not so with Jesus. In his first sermon in Luke, he treads into very unsafe territory. Jesus is preaching at the synagogue in his hometown; a place where he probably had attended as a parishioner for many years. His sermon, scarcely a few sentences in length, made quite an impression. After that first sermon, his parishioners tried to throw him over the hill. Now, I have had seen some negative reactions to sermons through the years, but never have I seen a congregation try to throw the preacher over the hill!

What led to this rash act? Jesus described stories in the sacred texts where God didn't always show favor to Israel. Jesus told them two stories from the prophets when Gentiles were healed and not the children of Israel. He said, "There were plenty of lepers in Israel in the time of Elisha the prophet, and none of them were healed . . . only Naaman, a Syrian."

That did it. Not his claim of being Messiah. It was when he told them the Messiah of their God wasn't just theirs alone. God was going to bless those "other people." Those other people who were enemies. Those Gentiles. That was when the crowd went into a rage.

## MORGAN'S RESPONSE TO "WELCOME TO LUKE"

This sermon is a fine exposition of the text, so I'm wondering if we can give it more of a bite at the end. At the end, go back to your candidating sermon and say, "I'm wondering what would have happened if I had followed Jesus' example when I delivered my candidating sermon. What if I had given it a non-controversial title, something like, "Amazing Grace," but then launched into the sermon with an opening sentence that said, 'God's grace is so amazing that the only way we can understand its breadth is by realizing that God loves George Bush, Bill Clinton, Osama bin Laden, Adolf Hitler, Charles Manson and Billy Graham . . . all of them . . . in the very same way. If I had followed the reading of the scripture lesson with that opening remark, would I be standing here today? What would your reaction have been? I'm sure you wouldn't have tried to throw me over a hill, but maybe you might have invited me to go back over the hill and out of town. What is your inner reaction to that statement right now, even after all these years in which you've gotten to know me and realize that I'm not some kind of a nut? What is it that I would need to clarify about such a statement as you reflect upon the impossibility of putting all those utterly different personalities in the same room and listening to their conflicts with one another?

And yet it is such an incredibly impossible love of God that Luke wants us to be thinking about. In his collection of Jesus' parables, he will be telling us that God loves each one of us with the same universal, unlimited, unmerited, uncalculating, and unconditional love.

I don't believe I ever preached those words Morgan recommended. I might have made some reference to God loving Hitler the same way God loves Billy Graham. But I wasn't ready to put all those characters in the same room, engage my congregation in imagining their conflicts, and proclaim God's love for them, a love that overwhelmed all the hate and hurt and mass destruction that existed there in the room with them.

When Morgan sent me those words, our nation was hurtling into a series of mass shootings that have now become a public health crisis. Throughout our descent into these times, most of our citizens, pastors included, have been hesitant to tell it like it is because of the fear of offending somebody. I have been one of that majority. What would happen if we placed that hesitation aside and took the risk of being thrown off the cliff by an angry congregation?

Preaching is an act of trust. When I stand behind the communion table to deliver my sermon, I am invited by God to tell it like it is. With each sermon every week, I am invited to speak boldly.

The gospel is bold, cutting through the waffling and threatening talk that fills the air around it. The gospel is bracing and powerful enough to get someone killed (after all, we are followers of a man who was crucified) and gracious enough to overturn the evil powers that claim us. In these perilous times of deeper and deeper division, Morgan's challenge still stands in my heart: "What if . . . ?"

The question of speaking truth in a powerful way was one of the biggest challenges I faced as a preacher. That challenge came during challenging times in our nation. During the years I served as a pastor, our nation became much more polarized and violent.

In January 2015, ten years after I began preaching, the pope spoke out about the Charlie Hebdo killings in France. He said, "killing in the name of religion is an aberration." But he also added "those who deride other faiths can expect to provoke a strong . . . even violent . . . response."[1] In one statement the Pope both denounced the attack by two militant Muslims and described Charlie Hebdo's satire as stepping over the line in its raunchy and mordant depiction of the Prophet Muhammad.

In those days, calling a person a terrorist was a common rebuke in our nation. The label "terrorist" was aimed at a wide variety of targets ranging from persons who disagreed with us to those who planned or enacted acts of violence. Who is a terrorist? When I wrote a sermon that January on the story of Jonah and sent it to Morgan I said, "This one is a bit firmer than many of my sermons. Please warn me if I am getting preachy. I hope I haven't stepped over the line in this one." Here is a portion of that sermon:

## SERMON PORTION: "IN THE SEASON OF OUR HATRED"

Many biblical scholars have described the story of Jonah as a warning to Hebrews who, as a result of their exile, had developed a spirit of bitterness toward other nations. They saw those other nations as their enemies. The story of Jonah begins with God asking Jonah to go to Nineveh,

1. Ball, "Pope Francis Sees Limits," para. 1.

"that great city," and tell the people to repent from their evil ways. Nineveh was the image of evil incarnate to the Hebrews in those days. It was the flourishing capital of Assyria, the nation that conquered the northern kingdom. Home of the evil King Sennacherib. The book of Nahum is devoted to prophetic denunciations against Nineveh. The king of Nineveh bragged about filling his city with the corpses of Hebrews. Of Judah, the king said, "I shut up King Hezekiah in Jerusalem like a caged bird. I plundered his cities and cut him off from his land."[2]

The audience of the story of Jonah were the people who had been part of those plundered cities. They had suffered horribly and mightily because of Assyria and Nineveh. Yet, we find God asking Jonah to go to that evil place and ask the people to repent. Jonah didn't go. He turned tail and ran the opposite direction. His fleeing led to a shipwreck and to his being swallowed by a big fish.

About that time, the Hebrew audience hearing this story would probably be applauding. "Good," they might say. The Hebrews who told and heard this story probably agreed that Nineveh was an evil city.

But God didn't agree, and God wasn't done with Jonah yet. In chapter 3, we find God asking Jonah a second time, "Go to Nineveh, that great city. Tell the people to repent" (Jonah 3:2). This time Jonah went. He preached a five-word sermon that didn't even mention God, and all the people repented. Jonah was furious.

In chapter 4, we find Jonah sulking on a hill overlooking Nineveh. Jonah confessed to God why he was reluctant to go to Nineveh in the first place. He said, "I knew you were a gracious God and merciful, slow to anger, and abounding in steadfast love, and ready to relent from punishing" (Jonah 4:2). In other words, Jonah knew that God would be gracious to Nineveh, and forgive those evil people. Jonah could not tolerate that. The story ends with Jonah sitting on that hill, fuming and fretting. We don't know if he was ever able to forgive the evil city of Nineveh—or God.

2. Pritchard, Ancient Near Eastern Texts, 288.

What does Jonah's story teach us? It teaches us that we must beware of our hatred and prejudices. The French hatred for the Muslims? How different is that hatred from Jonah's hatred of Nineveh? Not much. Our hatred of terrorists, at home or abroad? How different is that hatred from Jonah's hatred of Nineveh? Not much at all.

## MORGAN'S RESPONSE TO "IN THE SEASON OF OUR HATRED"

I think it's time to speak out about our reaction to terrorism, and you've described the terrorist context of the Jonah perfectly. There was every reason to hate Nineveh. Nineveh went far beyond our present-day terrorists in its brutality toward the people of the Northern Kingdom. And you've described Jonah's reluctance perfectly, noting that the average Hebrew would applaud his reluctance to offer repentance to Nineveh. Worse yet was the response of Nineveh: the people repented; but did not convert to Judaism! Not one person began worshipping Yahweh; no one was circumcised. Jonah came away from his preaching mission with not a single convert! Jonah had every reason to be angry. (The audience is still applauding his anger at this point!) It sounds like God was "soft on terrorists."

Now be careful when you get to the paragraph where you make comparisons with our current situation. Yes, ask the questions, but don't give answers. For example, "What does the Book of Jonah say about our hatred and anger toward Muslim terrorists, at home or abroad? (Don't mention the war on terror because it leads into the related question of our right to defend ourselves and that's not what we can deal with in this sermon—stick to our anger. And don't answer your questions with, "Not much. Not much at all." Let your hearers supply the answers) Move on and state, "If we think the Book of Jonah is hopelessly idealistic and impractical and that it simply does not apply to our present situation, then what do we make of Jesus' command to love our enemies?

Jesus said that in circumstances worse than ours today. He said this to a people whose country was occupied by foreign armies, the armies of the Roman Empire. He was speaking to people who had their backs against the wall, people who had no army, people who were being taxed into poverty, people who were crucified then left on the cross to putrefy for days as examples (thousands of them) when they resisted! So how do we deal, not only with Jonah, but with Jesus and his impossible commandment to love our enemies?"

By bringing Jesus into the discussion, we are offering a real challenge to the fear and anger of our time. Let your hearers struggle with it. If they confront you as they leave church, all you need to say is, "So, what does it mean to love these enemies? What would you tell Jesus? Your argument is not with me but with Jesus. He's the One to whom we'll have to answer some day." That's really my only suggestion: that you bring Jesus into the challenge. The rest of the sermon is fine. You'll get some flack, but that goes with the territory assigned to us.

I had to take a breath after reading Morgan's words. He pressed on a tender spot in my conscience. I had already noticed my own discomfort when I asked him, "I don't want to get preachy." When I was writing this sermon, I remember drifting into one of my high and mighty attitudes. There was a terrible eagerness in the writing, an eagerness that urged me to preach at something or someone. Such eagerness is always a warning to me that my pride and need to be right were holding sway.

But my deepest learning from Morgan was to question whether Americans and this American preacher had any right to compare ourselves with the Hebrew people in Jonah's day. We are not like the Hebrews. We are not like the poor people Jesus healed and taught. We are the privileged. We are the ones who build the walls to keep people out, spend more in a day than many spend in a year, enjoy the protection of an ocean that has keep wars far away from us. Nine-eleven was our wake-up call, but the suffering of 9/11 was a mosquito bite compared with the suffering of many other people in the world. It's not about terror, it's about our anger, our outrage.

We might be angry, but we are not a people whose backs are against the wall, a people who have no army, a people who are taxed into poverty.

I have always looked askance at Jonah. How childish of him, sulking on top of that hill, complaining about the heat and shaking his fist at God. But before I could step in front of my congregation to speak about Jonah, I had to find out that I was the one who needed to repent. I was the one who was like Jonah. I was the one who needed to let go of my need to be right and let God be right for a change. I had to take my preaching conversation to Jesus just as I was asking my congregation to do. Each day, I must make that same choice. The need to judge and be right has never left me. So, before I go off the rails into a terrible eagerness to preach at my enemies, I must search for the voice of Jesus.

Only then, when I step over the line of correctness and must take the heat, can I claim I walk the journey of Jesus and accept the consequences of what goes with the territory.

CHAPTER EIGHT

# The Live Performance

I BEGAN WATCHING MY sermons on video six years after starting ordained ministry. In my first year with the church in Elgin, Illinois, I married my husband, Dan. Dan is Jewish. We were able to have our wedding under a *chuppah* at the Presbyterian church where I was pastor. The congregation welcomed him, and Dan began doing video recordings of my sermons a few years later. I am forever grateful to First Presbyterian for allowing Dan to do this. Seeing the sermon "live" is essential to learning and improving. A sermon is a living event experienced at a specific time in a specific place by those who are present. A manuscript is a document, not an experience that is shared by those gathered to worship God.

On the days Dan filmed the sermon, I would try to watch the video of the sermon as soon as I returned home while it was still fresh in my mind. Usually I had a sense of how well I did. I also could vividly remember the portions of the manuscript I had forgotten. The experience of watching myself live was very unsettling. I didn't like the way I looked. I didn't like the way I moved my body. I didn't like my facial expressions or how my voice sounded, and on and on.

But I kept watching the sermon videos. The process of watching them helped me to correct the obvious problems I saw. But the bigger problems refused to yield. In the meantime, I began to send those videos to Morgan. Here is his response to one of those first videos (see the video on https://www.mentoringwithmorgan.com/resources/).

## *MORGAN'S RESPONSE TO "LIKE THOSE WHO DREAM"*

Regarding the December 27th video, your freedom from your manuscript is flawless. My general impression, however, is that you emphasized almost every sentence, as some Sunday School teachers try to hold the attention of children by emphasizing every point. If every sentence is emphasized, how will we know the main point? I felt that you needed to move along as you tell your story, and then, at the main point, make your emphasis. Your opening story was great, emphasizing almost physically, as well as verbally, your frustration that day in the hospital. After that, however, you needed to decide where to emphasize your main points, then move along to the next one. At any rate, that was my impression.

Here I was, seven years into ordained ministry, and still I would stand up every Sunday morning and forget parts of the sermon manuscript! This problem didn't become obvious until Morgan began to watch the sermon videos. We had managed to work well together to construct a good sermon on paper, but when those sermons were delivered, not all those words were preached. And what was I doing when I wasn't preaching? I was circling back to the parts I *could* remember, while I tried to find my place in the manuscript. I was wandering in the wilderness, and those who were listening were wandering with me and asking themselves, "Where is she going? What point is she trying to make?" While all of this was going on, I was still up there in front; but I was in a mild panic, looking for some landmark in the manuscript to grab so I could finish the sermon.

I had been coping this way for seven years. In those years, I did a good job of writing my sermons two to three weeks ahead. I whispered them fifteen times the night before I preached, but I still forgot portions of every sermon. When I told Morgan about these episodes, he was very surprised. "I don't know what I would do if I didn't know what the next sentence was supposed to be," he said. I, on the other hand, kept making it up as I went along, hoping I would find my way to the end and land the aircraft at some airport, not in some obscure field.

I had worked so hard, and yet I was still struggling to swim in the water of preaching without a manuscript. It was one of the most discouraging episodes in my long journey with Morgan. Discovering this problem led me into a whole new world of preaching.

But before we journey into that world, let's look at that sermon Morgan described as "teachy." As you watch the video, I invite you to try to follow the video in the following sermon manuscript. You will run into a few surprises!

## SERMON MANUSCRIPT: "LIKE THOSE WHO DREAM"

Years ago, I took my father to Barnes Hospital in St. Louis. He called me when I was working in Detroit, telling me he was suffering from jaundice. One of the doctors in his small-town hospital had called him and told him he had cancer and he was going to die. I was appalled. Dad hadn't had any tests that would confirm a cancer diagnosis. So, I arranged an ambulance that would take him to St. Louis, and I met him there after his first test. There were many more tests scheduled for the rest of the week.

At the end of my first day at Barnes, I went downstairs to the lobby. I had rushed out of Detroit, stuffing a pile of Post-It notes into my purse that had the car and hotel arrangements written on them. As I sat in the lobby, I opened my purse and all the Post-It notes fell into a pile on the floor. Suddenly, the full impact of what I was dealing with hit me. My dad was sick, maybe dying. I was alone here. No one else from my family was with me. Then, I couldn't find the address of my hotel, and wouldn't know how to get there if I did. I felt terrified and alone. Suddenly, quietly, I felt something I never expected to feel. I felt consoled. Comforted. In that moment I knew God was with me, as surely as I knew I was breathing, and my heart was beating. For the rest of that long week, the feeling of consolation came to me over and over. When it happened, I thought I was dreaming. But I wasn't. The touch of the Holy Spirit was more real than any dream. More real than life itself.

Our story for today is much like a dream. Luke transports us to the temple in Jerusalem. We see a poor couple approach the temple gates with their newborn infant. Then we see the priest Simeon at the door, letting them in.

My story of God's showing up at Barnes Hospital isn't unique. I have heard many stories like it, told to me by people of all ages, all faith traditions, and all circumstances. If you have had such an experience in your own life, I invite you to bring that moment into focus today as we visit Simeon and Anna the day they opened the temple door for Mary, Joseph, and Jesus.

Our story begins and ends in the temple precincts. Mary and Joseph brought their newborn child to the temple to fulfill Jewish law. Hebrew law instructed families to bring their child to be named, circumcised, and blessed eight days after being born. They also brought a sacrifice of two turtle doves to the temple. Since Mary and Joseph were poor, they could not afford to bring a lamb. Two turtledoves were considered appropriate for those of limited means.

We are in the temple, a holy place. A place where prayers are lifted to God. How lovely, how tender, the way aged Simeon cradles the infant Jesus in his arms. Imagine holding in your arms this most wanted child, the hope of the ages.[1] We are told that Simeon has been waiting for what Luke describes as the "consolation of Israel" his entire life. In those days, there was a deep longing for the coming of the Messiah. Many understood the Messiah as a military or political figure who would free the people from the oppression of Rome and rule with justice over Jerusalem.

---

1. Buttrick. *Interpreter's Bible*, 7:260.

But Simeon wasn't yearning for such a Messiah. He was yearning for God's consolation of Israel. He was looking for the promised journey home described by Jeremiah. "See, I am going to bring them from the north, and gather them from the farthest parts of the earth, a great company. They shall return to Jerusalem, with weeping they shall come, and with consolation I will lead them back."

Simeon wasn't looking for a conquering hero. He was looking for the healing only the presence of God could provide. He was looking for a restoration of God's covenant with the people, and for the healing of the rift between the Northern and Southern Kingdoms that occurred before the exile.

Simeon had been waiting all his life for this. When he gazed into the face of the infant Jesus, he knew. He knew that God had surely come and would restore the people who had walked in darkness for so many years. God came down, not to thrash evildoers or crush the Romans, but as an infant, to elicit love.

Have you ever noticed the kind of power infants have over adults? Men with calloused hands become gentle when handed a baby. People with gruff voices adopt a falsetto and coo to an infant. God came down as an infant to elicit love and nurture tenderness. For nurture and tenderness are the beginning of healing.

We are told that Simeon had waited all his life for this child, some 80 long years. And now that he had seen Jesus, he could die in peace. Simeon didn't need to stick around to see just how God's promises would be kept. His 80 years of waiting had taught him a valuable lesson. He had learned to trust God, and to continue to hope. He didn't scatter his thoughts and emotions along the landscape of worry and care. He waited, and he longed for one thing. Kierkegaard once said, "Purity of heart is to will one thing."[2] Jesus once said, "Blessed are the pure in heart, for they shall see God" (Matt 5:8).

Part of Simeon's vision of God were these arresting words: "Your salvation . . . is a light for revelation to the

---

2. Kierkegaard, *Purity of Heart*, loc. 19 of 2440.

Gentiles, and for glory to your people Israel" (Luke 2:30–32). God is not satisfied to allow the division between the Northern and Southern Kingdom stand. God is not satisfied to allow the division between the Jews and the Gentiles to stand. God is not satisfied to let any division of human creation divide the world God created.

So, God came as an infant, drawing out of all humanity the yearning, the tenderness, the comfort, and the hope that an infant can bring. For all things to be restored and Israel to be consoled, the hatred and fear and division must cease.

As you stand in the temple with me today, looking at Simeon's glowing face, ask yourself: "Is there one thing I long for, I yearn for in my life and my world? Is there one thing I want to see before I close my eyes?" Hold that thing in your heart in the light of the infant Jesus, resting in the arms of old Simeon.

Our God is a God of promises made and promises kept. And at the end of the day, we know that nothing can separate us from the love of God in Christ Jesus our Lord. My prayer for you in this New Year is that you might recognize where God is working and touching your life. My prayer for you is that like Simeon, you might have the blessing of seeing God in your moments and your days. Amen.

Did you discover the point I was making in the sermon in either the video or the manuscript? If you did, you have understood it better than I did—and I wrote it! The sermon story is an engaging one, but you may have noticed that the preached story is greatly expanded from the story in the manuscript. When I preach, I sometimes have a hard time getting started at the beginning of the sermon. When that happens, I spend more time in the opening story. By doing this, I try to make myself comfortable standing in front of the congregation. While such a practice might help me feel comfortable, it can be a deadly way to begin. A congregation needs to have something that grabs them and tells them they should keep listening. If a story goes too long, it loses its ability to hold their attention.

As the sermon begins, we are introduced to Simeon. We are told he is waiting for the consolation of Israel. But what does this mean? At this point in the sermon, you probably noticed I circled back several times to the image of Simeon. This is the place where I forgot the manuscript. I didn't find my way back until I mentioned Kierkegaard. Then, the image of waiting for one thing appeared again. Is that to be the point of the sermon? Or is the sermon trying to reassure us in our waiting? Or perhaps, encourage us to see God in our waiting? Although I found myself and the manuscript at the end of the sermon, I didn't provide closure. As Morgan would say, the sermon managed to take off, but it never really landed.

The teachy tone Morgan described was the sound of a distracted person who had forgotten her sermon and was desperately trying to find her way. I was trying to keep myself (and the congregation) occupied while I searched for the point or my place in the manuscript.

How could I learn to remember the sermon, the whole sermon? The first step in my search for an answer to this question was in Morgan's "Steps to Improved Preaching," which are the focus of the following chapter. The step that most pertains to this situation is *Rule Two*.

CHAPTER NINE

# Morgan's Steps to Improved Preaching

IN THE LAST YEAR of my short time on the faculty at Louisville Presbyterian Theological Seminary, I was asked to teach a course entitled Advanced Preaching Practicum. The professor of homiletics had to be away during that term and, thus, I was asked to take over his class. There were only a few students who signed up for the class (which may say something about the low esteem in which preaching is held by many of today's seminarians), and what I learned was they were in need of something more basic than what would be described as an advanced class on homiletics. Sometime toward the end of the semester, I gave them a short list of practical guidelines entitled *Morgan's Steps to Improved Preaching.* Since that time, I have reduced the number of those steps from eleven to eight by combining those that belong together. However, I will also be enlarging upon these strategies that I hope will be helpful to any preacher who is seeking improvement in the preparation and delivery of sermons. So, here we go!

## *RULE ONE*

I am beginning with this step because it is the most important lesson I ever learned about preaching. *Write for the ear, as if you were a composer of music.* As you prepare your sermon, remember you are not writing for readers, but for listeners. Even if your church publishes printed versions of your sermon, remember your sermon is not a paper to be delivered as a lecture. A sermon is, first, something that happens live on Sunday morning. Write as though Sunday morning is your only chance to deliver your message. As you write, learn to hear each sentence as you write it. It may help to whisper every sentence to yourself.

This may be a difficult discipline to develop. In this age of word processing, most of us are typing our sermons, and if we learned touch-typing in high school, we are writing at a very rapid rate. Also, we still carry with us the unconscious need to please our professors with what we write, and thus we write for the eye, rather than for the ear. I learned how to hear what I was writing because of an interesting accident.

One Sunday afternoon in the early years of my ministry, I was going over the manuscript I had typed on an old-fashioned Royal portable. It was late afternoon, and this sermon was to be delivered at a service that evening. Feeling a bit fatigued, I got up and walked about the front room of this old manse in which the church housed us, reading my sermon as I did. At one point, I leaned on the mantle of the fireplace (it was no longer in use and had been boarded up as a solid wall). Holding my sermon in my right hand near the wall above the mantle, I did not notice there was a small crack between the mantle and the wall, the result of many years in which this old manse had been neglected. For some reason, the manuscript slipped from my hand through the crack, disappearing into the wall where it could not be retrieved. (It is probably still there until this day, awaiting future discovery as in the story of how Hilkiah discovered "the book of the law" during Josiah's repair of the temple [2 Kgs 22]. When mine is discovered, it will probably not lead to a great reformation as in the days of Josiah.)

What was I to do? I would have to preach in two hours, and my manuscript was lost! Going to my desk, I wrote what I could remember on a yellow legal pad. As I did this, I made myself hear every sentence, and noticed how the energy of my handwriting reflected the emphasis needed on certain words. Even though this was last-minute preparation, the delivery of the sermon that evening went well, and so I decided to write my sermon for the following Sunday on that same yellow pad. For the next thirty years, every one of my sermons was handwritten! And as this was done, I was always hearing my sermon as I wrote each sentence.

Many years later, when I acquired my first computer, I wondered if I could make a transition from writing sermons by hand to typing them. Fearing I might lose my developed ability to hear each sentence, I spent the entire summer writing sermons both by hand and by typing. What I learned was I could make the transition to typing. But it was possible only because of my thirty years of writing by hand.

Recently, I have learned that two of my favorite authors, David McCullough and Wendell Berry, write only by hand. Berry writes,

> As a farmer, I do almost all of my work with horses. As a writer, I work with a pencil or a pen and a piece of paper. My wife types my work on a Royal standard typewriter bought new in 1956 and as good now as it was then . . . . She is my best critic because she is the one most familiar with my habitual errors and weaknesses . . . . We have, I think, a literary cottage industry that works well and pleasantly.[1]

So, remember that sermons, like music, are composed for listeners, not for readers. Maybe try writing your next sermon by hand—you may like it!

### RULE TWO

After completing your exegetical homework on the text, develop a written flight plan for your sermon. State the sermon's purpose or

---

1. Berry, *What are People For?*, 179.

goal in one sentence. When asked by a student how many points a sermon should have, a homiletics professor once answered, "At least one!" If you can't state your purpose or goal in one sentence, work on it until you can. The advantage in following this simple rule is it will keep you on track as you prepare the sermon. As you write the sermon, you can evaluate all your material by asking if it is taking your listeners in the direction of your stated goal. It may also help you arrive at the most fitting title for the sermon. In arriving at a title, ask yourself a simple question: If this title were posted on an outdoor church bulletin board, would it be sufficiently interesting to cause someone driving by to come and hear the sermon? Most of our sermon titles fail to pass this test. In the first edition of these steps, I restated this need for a flight plan by saying, "Better a short flight that lands at some airport than a long one that crashes in a country field."

## *RULE THREE*

Always finish the writing of your manuscript by Thursday evening *at the very latest*. Better yet, prepare your manuscript a week, or even two weeks, before the date of delivery. This will sound like an impossible practice to those preachers who delay their preparation until Saturday. However, the great advantage in such prior preparation is it gives you more time for revision. The more you return to your manuscript over a week or two, the more you will discover what needs to be changed. It's never too late to add, cut, and rearrange right up to the moment of delivery.

So, revise, revise, revise. I followed this rule about the importance of revision so consistently I would often revise the sermon I had preached in the first service before delivering it in the second service. My manuscripts ended up looking rather messy because of all the little revisions I had jotted down in the margins, but such constant revision produces results. One of the other ways in which I would engage in such revision was by carrying the manuscript in my pocket and reading it in all kinds of odd places, sometimes sitting on a bench in a shopping center on a Saturday afternoon.

If you are wondering how you will ever discipline yourself to work a week or two in advance of the delivery date, the answer is simple: during some vacation or study leave time, write two or three sermons. Be sure to get something down on paper. With those two or three sermons in hand, you can then stay on this schedule of advance preparation.

## *RULE FOUR*

As Sunday approaches, read (or whisper) your sermon at least twelve (maybe even fifteen) times before preaching it. Become a sermon whisperer until you develop the skill of hearing in your head what you have written without having to whisper it. As you read and revise your sermon, underline important words in color. Delete what doesn't belong, or scribble new wording in the margins. This will help you to see paragraphs and pages in your mind.

## *RULE FIVE*

Give serious attention to the beginning and ending of your sermon. Remember the opening sentences of your sermon are *very* important. Because we live in an era of short attention spans, you have only about three minutes to convince your listeners to stay tuned. Try to picture every person in the congregation holding a remote control. You need to convince them not to go channel surfing for something more interesting, so deliver your opening words with great care. At the same time, be sure the ending of your sermon is carefully prepared. When you arrive at your destination, land immediately. Don't keep circling the airport. As a preacher once remarked to me, "Always drive in the right-hand lane so you don't miss your exit."

## *RULE SIX*

Develop freedom from your manuscript, after all, you wrote it! The sanctuary is not a classroom. A sermon is your personal testimony of how Scripture has spoken to your heart, so work to make your delivery reflect such a heartfelt message.

## RULE SEVEN

Don't allow sermon preparation to isolate you from your people. Time spent in pastoral or hospital visitation is as important as time spent in sermon preparation. George Arthur Buttrick, pastor of the Madison Avenue Presbyterian Church of New York City, and arguably one of the finest preachers of the twentieth century, spent his afternoons in pastoral visitation—and it had to be done by bus or subway! It has been said the preacher who is invisible to his people during the week will probably be incomprehensible on Sunday.[2] Spending time with your people will make a difference in your preaching. By being with them regularly, you will be reminded you're preaching to real people. It will rescue you from quotations that are scholarly, showy, and pedantic—the kind that are comprehensible to seminary graduates, but not to everyday folks. Quotations that are meaningful for you may not be easily digested by your people, so avoid such quotations. Remember what was said of the preaching of Jesus, that "the common people heard him gladly" (Luke 4:15). So, don't try to be more eloquent than Jesus!

## RULE EIGHT

Remember you *can* be a better preacher. You have not been called to an impossible task. When Dean Roberts reached the end of our final class in Senior Homiletics, he gave us an important and encouraging word for the future. We needed such a hopeful word; here we were facing forty years of future ministry, wondering how we could possibly produce a decent sermon on every Sunday morning for the rest of our ministerial life. And so, he said to us, "It ought not to be all that difficult to speak lovingly about your Lord for twenty minutes each week." That is, after all, what preaching is about: sharing with your people every week some simple good word for Jesus. You wouldn't be

2. Buttrick, *Preaching Jesus Christ*, 83.

in the ministry if you didn't believe that Jesus, the Christ, is such good news. So, think of your weekly sermon in that way. For that matter, as you work at these steps, you may want to deliver shorter sermons, maybe just fifteen minutes will do, because I've never known a congregation that complained about short sermons. One good, short word for Jesus every week will have people telling you, "That sermon spoke to me today. Give us more next week!"

# CHAPTER TEN

# Becoming the Sermon

During my years of preaching, I would tell my husband Dan that all the study time I spent on Saturday nights was "pickling." A sermon manuscript on paper is a cucumber. By the time I had to stand up and preach it both the sermon and I had to be a pickle. The seasoning of the words of the sermon, the longings of my heart, and the mystery of what God intends must seep into my very being.

As the years went by, I realized the analogy had to go even further. By the time I had to stand up and preach, I had to reveal my true self and become the words I preached. The act of preaching is an incarnational act, a tiny version of the gospel mystery of "the word became flesh" (John 1:14).

The answer to the question "Why do I forget parts of my sermon every week?" was those parts either never belonged in the first place, or they were not incorporated into my deepest self. If preaching is incarnation, the question "Does she really believe what she is saying?" is answered as the words the preacher speaks, her gestures, her tone of voice, and her presence are experienced by the congregation and the preacher together. During the preaching event, the Christ in the preacher is seeking to connect with the Christ in the hearers. The preacher is only an instrument, willingly playing the music God is providing.

How does one become the sermon? In my experience, it isn't done by sheer will power or some magic bullet technique. In those darkest days when I was forgetting every week, I despaired I would never be able to preach by heart. On those days, I was reminded of the words of Paul, "Work out your own salvation with fear and trembling, for it is God who is at work in you" (Phil 2:12–13). I clung to the hope the God who began a good work in me would see that work to its completion. I had to learn to keep depending on those promises of God. And I had a mentor who was tirelessly helping me week in and week out, coaxing along the process of learning and encouraging me. Morgan never gave up on me. God never gave up on me. So, who was I to throw in the towel?

During this period of more than three years where I was forgetting sermons and sounding teachy, there was one breakthrough. It happened when I was working on the Easter sermon for 2014. I sent Morgan an email with a plea: "Help! What more can a preacher say about the resurrection?"

## MORGAN'S RESPONSE

Real resurrection is always about going home, but not "going back." Resurrection always takes us forward to our real home. What many of the exiles in Babylon were hoping for was a return to the way things had been in the past. Their eventual behavior in the Second Temple proves that they had failed to get the point. They went back to their old ways, so eventually the Second Temple was destroyed, just like the first. What God wanted was a renewed Israel, the kind of holy nation that would be a blessing to the world. Instead of that, Israel betrayed its calling and became a nation in which its own poor were oppressed, a nation to which God sent prophets to recall it to righteousness. The return from Babylon was a chance to start all over again and "do it right" but it didn't happen.

So, what is the lesson in all of this? When we think of resurrection and homecoming, what do we expect? When we've experienced the loss of a job, financial disaster, the death of a loved one, what does it mean to experience resurrection and homecoming? Obviously, God isn't going to bring back our loved ones who have died. But neither does it mean that God is going to re-fresh our bank account and find the perfect job for us. "Going to heaven" won't be a homecoming to our former comforts, a reunion of our crowd and all the good times we had in the old days. We need to get all these fake im-ages of resurrection out of our minds.

The only real home to which God can bring us is our true self, the self that God created us to be. Until we realize this, we go on hoping that our false self has some kind of future, which it doesn't. We sometimes think that our body image, our success, our education, our clothes and cars, our money and our job constitute our identity. But that's not who we really are. This is the self that we have created in our minds, but it has no future. God can't raise all our stuff from the dead. We can't carry all that stuff with us into the Father's house. Maybe the ups and downs of life are supposed to urge us onward to the dis-covery of our real self. If all we have at the end of life is that false self, there is nothing for God to "eternalize."

The only "me" that God can raise from the dead is the "real me," and God will never give up on our real, true self. One reason why I believe in universal salvation is that I believe that the real me and the real you can never die. God will never give up on His original plan for our life; that original design is what God can raise from the dead . . . and God will accomplish that if it takes all of eternity.

Real resurrection and homecoming are painful. Learning to become who I really am involves giving up my idolatry of my false self and all its stuff. Learning to take all the trappings of my false stuff lightly requires genuine humility. I will continue to value my education and ordination, but I know that in the Father's house, I will cease to be Reverend Dr. F. Morgan Roberts, D.D, LL. D, etc. I'll just be Morgan, but a much more genuine Morgan than you or I have ever known.

As I learn to enjoy being just me, I'll learn to en-joy the other real, little people who have experienced resurrection and homecoming. My friend Joom, the little Asian lady who walks in our neighborhood every morning, will be a creature of eternal splendor in that resurrection world, even though everyone ignores her now.

For now, however, resurrection is a painful exercise, maybe a bit like the good kind of painful we experience when we first decide to get our bodies into shape. The pain of real resurrection will be deeply painful. God will have to use failure to bring us home to our true self. That's why one poet has described this joyful pain by writing, "Then you will know how marvelous it is to live threatened with resurrection."[1] Real resurrection is life-threatening!

I was stunned the night I read these words. It is a night I will never forget. Although part of me already knew the words Morgan sent, I had to descend to a deeper knowing. This knowing involved surrender, something I had managed to shun. I had to give the sermon back to God, trust that God's excavation project to revive the person God created me to be would bear fruit, and, finally, be a resurrection. "God will never give up on His original plan for our life; that original design is what God can raise from the dead . . . and God will accomplish that if it takes all of eternity." Those words sent chills through my whole body, and that night I knew this was the one thing I had been seeking my whole life.

I sent the following reply,

> Dear Morgan,
>
> We lost so many members of the church last year. They were glorious people who shared their gifts with us for decades. Today I walked up the quiet steps of the funeral home down the street and I saw the outline of a woman just turned 80. She lost her husband yesterday. Her children are out of town. Grandchildren too. She is alone, sitting in front of the large desk of the funeral home director.
>
> Her solitary sorrow almost knocked me over. Steeling all the strength I could muster, I walked in. She smiled and reached out to touch me. "Here you are!" she said. I

---

1. Esquivel, *Threatened with Resurrection*, 63.

sensed how important my presence was, and I quaked again. Yes, I am threatened by the resurrection. I know there is something beyond these dark funeral home days. I have even glimpsed bits of it.

The resurrection has taught me that I must keep journeying. The hurt is a good hurt. It is giving me a bigger heart. It is removing armor I have created to protect myself. I feel the pain more deeply with each death and every riven thing[2] that just must go because it really isn't "me."

I am glad to have this journey with you. Years and years of learning. It is a gift beyond words, beyond deserving. It is a gift of companionship, humanity, and grace. A gift of God.

### EASTER SERMON TEXT: HOLD ON![3]

A three-year-old, new to his Sunday school class, had just finished singing "Jesus Loves Me." As the class was being dismissed, he came up to his Sunday school teacher and asked, "Is Jesus here?" The teacher paused for a moment. She wasn't sure if she should say, yes Jesus is here and leave it at that, or explain to him that yes, we can feel that Jesus is here. Before she had time to reply, he asked again, "Is Jesus here, because I can't see his feet!"

I guess when you are three, feet are what you look for when you are trying to find a grown-up. But maybe this isn't only true for a three-year-old. In our story for today, two women at the tomb encounter Jesus as they are running away to tell the disciples that the tomb was empty. When they ran into him, they did something very interesting. They held on to his feet.

Matthew's story of the resurrection is the most dramatic story we find in the gospels. Two women came to the tomb Easter morning to mourn his death. They had probably heard that the Roman soldiers had sealed the

2. Winman, Christian, "Every Riven Thing."

3. Sermon video on mentoringwithmorgan.com

tomb with a huge stone and posted guards outside, so they weren't planning on trying to anoint the body. They were there to quietly mourn.

Then there was an earthquake. An angel appeared, rolled back the stone, and sat upon it. The soldiers became frozen in fright. The angel then announced that Jesus wasn't there and invited the women to peer into the tomb so they could see for themselves. Then the angel told them to tell the disciples that Jesus had gone ahead of them into Galilee.

As they turned from the grave and ran, they literally ran into Jesus. Recognizing him right away, they grabbed his feet. The Greek verb for grab means "to seize." Matthew uses that word one other time earlier in the story, the time the soldiers seized Jesus to bring him to trial.

Grabbing on to the leg or feet of a beloved parent is something children do quite often. If that parent is acting like they might leave or do something the child doesn't want, the child will grab on. "Daddy don't leave!" is often followed by an arm wrapped around Daddy's leg. When I imagine our resurrection story today, I can almost see those two women grabbing on to Jesus for dear life. "Where are you going now? You have already dragged us all the way to Jerusalem, and then you got yourself killed and put in a tomb; let's stay here for a while."

On every Easter Sunday of our lives, we see Jesus escaping again. Escaping our grasp, escaping the tombs of the world, escaping to all the Galilees of our lives. The minute we start to bask in the wonder, love and praise of the glorious resurrection,[4] we find the whole reality of Jesus' life escaping from our grasp.

"Is Jesus here, because I can't see his feet!?"

Today, as we allow the resurrection to sink in, I invite you to ask yourself a question: "If we believed in the resurrection, how would our lives and world be different?"

As you roll that question over in your mind, I will share with you some of my reflections. Perhaps together

4. Wesley, "Love Divine, All Loves Excelling," 366.

we can learn to let the reality of the resurrection speak to us.

If we believed in the resurrection, how would life be different? For starters, it would mean that God is sovereign. The resurrection is the trademark of the power of God. It is evidence that the sovereignty of God is true sovereignty. God is no small monarch reigning over a graveyard. Death in not the real king. God is not a local deity ruling under the power of death. God is sovereign.

Generally, we don't realize just how much death reigns in our minds and hearts. It is hard for us to even imagine a body that doesn't deteriorate, a world that does not threaten death to many of its people, a planet that doesn't have species dying, a world where people are all part of one family.

Death is the trump card that all the powers that be use to keep people in check. Death is the reason we grasp and grab. The reason we clutch. We clutch our assets, fearfully build oversized estates to demonstrate our superiority, and maintain a fierce grip on our positions as though the loss of them would mean the loss of our very self. If there were no death, what would we have to lose? Jesus is talking about a world where death itself is left behind. When God raised Jesus from the dead, a whole new kind of life began. Resurrection life. And resurrection life is a threat to everything that clings to our death-dealing world.

If we believed in the resurrection, how would life be different? The powers that be would no longer be the powers that be. In Jesus' day, the powers that be were the Roman government and the chief priests. Together, those powers had the poor under their thumb. Those two groups were so threatened by the rumor that resurrection might happen, they sealed the tomb with a huge stone and posted armed guards to secure it. They couldn't take the chance that even a rumor of resurrection might get out of that tomb, much less the risen Lord.

Why? Because they knew that the resurrection would empower the poor in ways they could only imagine. Nothing would stop the little people from working for God's purposes. They would be eager to work for

God's promises of justice, peace and love that Jesus had taught them. They would be more daring to risk living fully and loving wastefully. More willing to share what they have with those who have nothing. More courageous in speaking out against the abuses of Caesar's empire and more ready to risk all for God's empire.

None of this would do. The threat of resurrection was a real threat then, and it continues to be. The poet Julia Esquivel understood that threat in her work in Guatemala. Her country endured nearly thirty years of political violence under the rule of a series of dictators. She watched as thousands and thousands of indigenous groups were savagely murdered. Hundreds of villages were literally wiped off the face of the earth.

Against that bloody backdrop, she said of those who lost their lives: "They have threatened us with resurrection because they are more alive than ever before, because they transform our agonies and fertilize our struggle, because they pick us up when we fall, because they loom like giants. That is the whirlwind which does not let us sleep, the reason why sleeping, we keep watch, and awake, we dream."[5]

You see, resurrection doesn't mean life as we know it will go on and on. Resurrection doesn't mean we get to go to heaven when we die. Resurrection means oh so much more than that! Resurrection means death will not have the final word. Resurrection means you don't need to spend your whole lifetime protesting death, asserting your strength against its grip, or striving to squeeze an eternity's worth of meaning, pleasure, security, and satisfaction from your diminishing life span. For, as you know, in that scenario, death still wins. Death still speaks its icy "No."

Resurrection means God has spoken a thunderous "Yes" to the life and ministry of Jesus, and to your life. When the moment of mortality tries to pronounce a grim "No" over your grave, death will be overwhelmed and overmatched by God's incomprehensible "Yes."

---

5. Esquivel, Julie, *Threatened by Resurrection*, 59.

So today, cling to his feet and experience the reality of resurrection life. And tomorrow, when you return to whatever Galilee you face each day, remember Jesus is alive and he is returning there with you with the astonishing miracle of his "Yes!"

Amen.

If you have listened to the video, you may have noticed I didn't forget any of the paragraphs in the manuscript. This was the first time that had ever happened. The paragraphs weren't in the manuscript anymore. They were grafted in my heart. I was finally preaching by heart.

CHAPTER ELEVEN

# Does Anyone Know
# What Happens to a Sermon?

On the afternoon of July 21, 2013, Dan and I left church and went to my favorite place to eat. Although I don't remember exactly what I said, Dan has told me I was very upset. I realized that day I had preached a good sermon, a sermon where I spoke with confidence. The title of the sermon was, "The Unhindered Kingdom." Dan was so impressed with the sermon, he later found images that he placed in the sermon video, putting pictures with the words.[1]

Why was I so upset? I was afraid I would never preach a sermon as good as that one ever again. I was afraid it was a fluke. Next week and the week after that I would drift back to forgetting, wandering in the wilderness, and landing in some remote field. On days like that Sunday afternoon I appreciated knowing I had a mentor, that I could call him, that he would still be there for the hard times, just as he had always been.

Turns out, the thing I needed to be worried about was the topic of the sermon, not its delivery. The sermon was about the kingdom of God. I had begun to hear from the congregation that they wanted more social justice sermons. I preached "The Unhindered Kingdom" in response to their voiced concerns. But it was

---

1. Video on mentoringwithmorgan.com.

not enough. I was able to articulate what hinders the kingdom, but I was still struggling with what to do to help *bring* the kingdom of God into our lives and our world. I would spend the rest of my days as a called pastor struggling with that question, right up until the final Sundays I would preach. And beyond! The seed of that struggle carried me beyond pastoral ministry and into the adventures of the next journey.

I began ministry at First Presbyterian one month after President Obama was elected. The years that followed were years when political polarization and horrible violence were increasing. When I began ministry there, I entered a church that had a history of acting on social justice issues in the sixties and seventies. But these times were different. My first attempt to lead the church into acting in our community on a social justice issue was to propose a gun give-back program where citizens could bring unwanted guns and ammunition to the police department and leave them there, no questions asked. Such a program had been done by the church in the 1980s, and I felt relatively confident we could do it again. But first, the session asked me to confer with the community pastor group. I asked that group of about twenty pastors if they would join me. Not one of them agreed. In fact, there was no real discussion. Each one said they would lose members if they participated. I was stunned into silence. Later, when I reported that meeting to the session, First Presbyterian decided not to sponsor such a program if no other church in our community would partner with us.

Later, at one of our session meetings, one elder proposed a letter be sent to the local newspaper in support of legislation described as "sensible gun laws." The heated discussion that followed resulted in a vote not to send the letter.

During those years, our denomination voted to allow the ordination of gay women and men into ministry. Churches in our regional presbytery began to leave, one by one. A couple of years later, our denomination voted to allow Presbyterian ministers to officiate marriages of same-sex couples. That action prompted unrest in many congregations, including the one I served. Some members considered leaving the church. While I had officiated at two civil union services early in my ministry there, many members were unaware of them because they had taken place in outdoor venues. Now that our denomination allowed pastors to officiate at these weddings, it was possible those services might happen in the sanctuary. While some members welcomed these developments, others were frightened and confused.

During this time, I was also being criticized for not preaching enough on the topic of social justice. I was standing squarely in the middle of groups of persons with conflicting views, and I ended up trying to please both. Where were my courageous words? How could they, as members, know how to respond to the world we lived in if I didn't take a clear stand on the issues of the day? Is that the role of a pastor? When does proclaiming the gospel end and talking politics begin?

When this all was going on, I asked Morgan what Jesus meant when he said the words, "thy kingdom come" (Matt 6:10). What was the kingdom of God?

## MORGAN'S RESPONSE

Whenever we preach about the kingdom of God it is important to make clear that there is no hard and fast boundary line between the present and future kingdom. If the fullness of God's kingdom will mean sharing by all and scarcity for none, then we must live in that eternal reality now. We must always be living in what George MacDonald called the Eternal Now, living today as we shall live forever in God's presence.[2] In the mind of Jesus there was no distinction between now and then. If we do not find our treasure today in those present moments in which we experience the joy of sharing our bread with the hungry, why would we want to live in some future kingdom in which all of the barriers between rich and poor are finally obliterated?

We must always be asking ourselves, "What are the moments in life that we treasure?" If we live, constantly awaiting a weekend-kind freedom from responsibility, a

2. MacDonald, *Gospel in George MacDonald*, 287.

time when we can get away from having to think about the needs of others, why would we want to spend eternity in God's perfect empire where those others are always with us? If we keep asking, "What do our hearts treasure?" we will begin to understand the meaning of Jesus' words: "What you treasure is your heart's true measure" (Matt 6:21).

This way of thinking about an unobstructed larger world in which the present and future have no boundary lines is, I am learning, a characteristic of the Enochic Judaism which formed the worldview of Jesus and the primitive church. Just this past week I came upon a passage in Margaret Barker's *The Lost Prophet: The Book of Enoch and its Influence on Christianity*. Regarding the notion of the kingdom of God, she writes, "If we allow ourselves to think in terms of dualism, time separate from eternity, we drive a wedge through the very heart of original gospel insight. We find ourselves with the idea of an 'eternal' life which starts only after physical death . . . with the idea that the Kingdom of God is something remote and unworldly. If we force ourselves back to the integrated worldview of the apocalyptists and the first Christians, we find that eternal life is earthly life already linked to and intersected with the other dimension, allowing what is beyond to suffuse and transform what is here."[3]

This primitive truth about our call to follow Jesus in his work of building the kingdom of God in our everyday life needs to be proclaimed as frequently and forcefully as we can. For most of our listeners, the idea of God's coming kingdom is something like the notion of the Final Great Retirement. When someone dies, we hear people consoling one another with the idea that "they have gone on to a better life." It is as though when our life ends, we move to a perfect gated community where we will no longer have to deal with those nasty people who have made life difficult for us in this world. It is a life of perfect rest and recreation, endless time to enjoy golf and bridge with our old friends.

3. Barker, *Lost Prophet*, 75.

However, in the Bible, we read of a city whose "gates are never shut (Rev. 21:25)," a city into which all are free to enter; not at all the kind of suburban retreat from reality that many people think of as heavenly. I honestly suspect that, if most of our members could see what an open city the final heavenly kingdom will be, they would decide that it is not at all the better life for which they hope. Indeed, such an open city in which the world's distinctions are gone forever, a kingdom in which we are no longer rich and the poor are no longer poor, a city in which the poor no longer need our largesse, would seem to be more like hell than heaven to many people.

So, we need to keep calling people to a life of watchfulness in which we look for those moments when the kingdom of God breaks in upon us, removing the barriers of injustice. We need to cultivate such moments as the true and lasting treasure of our lives. Just last week I was given such a moment. I was reading with Jonathan from a little book in which we read one sentence in English and then the same sentence in Spanish. Without his medication, Jonathan's OCD makes him a rather hyperactive child, but he seemed unusually calm and attentive on that day. Jonathan's three brothers also attend our school; his father is in prison, and his mother has married another man. For some reason, he was really enjoying himself, so much so that when the teacher announced that it was time to go to the spelling contest in the gathering area, he asked, "Couldn't we just stay in here and continue reading together?" Of course, we couldn't, but it was such a treasured moment to experience such oneness with one of God's dear children.

Such moments await anyone who wants to follow Jesus and enter God's kingdom today. If you can awaken your people to such "kingdom" moments, you will be giving them the only real and lasting treasure that can be found in life.

So that was it, no distinctions, everyone included. Such an arrangement would completely overturn the world as we know it. No competitive winner-take-all behavior. Everyone gets enough, has a home, is treated equally. No outcasts, no disparaging looks at those whose sexual orientation or gender identity is different. No 1 percent of the population holding 90 percent of the wealth. Everyone loved equally. No violence. Well, that image goes way beyond politics. It would be, literally, a new heaven and a new earth.

In the face of such a radical view, what is a person to do, day by day, week by week? Years went by, and my discomfort deepened. One thing that can happen to a sermon is it might change the preacher. As I opened my heart to the social justice issues that surrounded us, I became more and more uncomfortable with having people die almost every week in mass shootings.

How could I not speak directly about sensible gun laws? What was hindering me? Other pastors in mainline churches were facing these questions, too. Pastors were all looking at their individual situations: decline in membership, scarce financial resources, in some cases, even the survival of their churches. Our members were frightened too, afraid for the church to take a stand, for any stand would cause unrest in the church too. Fear was what was hindering the gospel. Our own fear of losing members or money, not surviving as a church or retaining an income, being criticized from within and without for speaking out.

That is when I began to realize preaching about social justice was not enough. I needed to get involved. I invited our session to participate in a community organization serving our local area. The leadership of the congregation declined to participate. But by now, the fire in my belly could not be quenched. Although the church did not join, I continued to be involved with a community organization and reported my activities to church members and leaders. During my final years of ministry, the Fox River Valley Initiative, part of the Chicago area Industrial Area Foundation, was able to redevelop a building with an over 110-year-old history that had closed in 2013 due to lack of funding. That building housed services for children for all those years before it closed. After it was redeveloped, it served persons in need of affordable housing and handicapped persons. I had stood on the lawn in front of that building in 2013, mourning yet another social service program that had shut down because of budget cuts. Before my ministry at First Presbyterian ended, I watched in wonder as our

City Council approved the proposal for affordable housing and housing for handicapped persons with no dissenting votes. Many people from my congregation participated in City Council meetings and some even told their story of working in that building when it was a school for emotionally disturbed children. Their joy shone as they watched the community preserve this historic landmark as a place where those in need would still be served. It was a glimpse of God's kingdom standing right there in their neighborhood. They were able to participate in something bigger than themselves, something that would help God's little people for years to come.

# CHAPTER TWELVE

# "Till We Come Round Right"[1]

AFTER THE APPROVAL OF the affordable and handicapped housing project in Elgin, there was a shooting that occurred only fifteen miles away from us. This time, instead of addressing this social justice issue on my own, I asked the session for volunteers to form a team of people to work with me on an educational event about the shooting. We would hold that event in our sanctuary, where we could provide a safe space for conversation. Such events held in public places sometimes ended in shouting matches and demonstrations. But in the sanctuary, participants could be reminded they were in a holy place.

The idea for the project began when I was asked to provide the invocation at the opening session of the Illinois General Assembly by our local representative. After I had helped with this task, I took that opportunity to ask her if we could have a meeting. Three members from the session and a member of another church in the community joined us. When the team met with our legislative representative, we decided to use a panel discussion format for our educational event. The team and I invited two congresspersons, the Kane County State's Attorney, our local Chief of Police, the chief from the community where the shooting took place, the Deputy Sheriff of the Illinois State Police, along with one of his directors,

1. Brackett, "Simple Gifts" (Shaker melody), v 1.

and the Kane County Sheriff. The preparation for this event was very challenging. We met with all the panel members to ask them to describe their understanding of the causes of the shooting, and what could be done to prevent such a shooting from occurring in the future. I consolidated all their responses into a report to the moderator of the event, and she used that material to choose questions to direct to the panel. We also invited those who attended the event to put their questions on index cards, and those questions were posed to the panel after a break. The evening was a wonderful success. Later, in a session meeting, those who were involved talked about how deeply meaningful our work had been. We had gone beyond writing checks. Our congregation that had been so generous for so many years in contributing financially to help those in need was finally able to get its feet wet in the real-world waters of doing social justice.

Before that event, when we were interviewing our community police chief, she questioned our team about why we were doing this.

"Don't you know how controversial this is? Why would a church do something like this?"

It was then that a member of our team pointed at me and said, "It was because of that sermon you preached. The one where you said, 'What are you going to do?'"

I couldn't believe my ears. One of my church leaders, who felt I didn't preach enough social justice in sermons, was pointing out a sermon as his inspiration for the panel discussion event.

I didn't know what sermon he was referring to. Finally, after a week of searching, I found it. It was a sermon I preached after the shooting at a mosque in New Zealand.

## SERMON PORTION: BE A CARETAKER

On Friday, a shooter walked into a mosque in Christchurch, New Zealand and opened fire. Then he moved on to another mosque. Further bloodshed was averted when a caretaker jumped on the gunman from behind and squeezed him so tight, he dropped his weapon. The caretaker must not have been familiar with guns, for he was unable to find the trigger. Perhaps he had never picked up a gun before. But that didn't stop him. He still chased the shooter away.

I remember several years ago, on the Sunday after Sandy Hook, several of you were dismayed that I didn't mention that incident during the sermon. I have had a few years to think about that decision, and today I want to reflect on both the children at Sandy Hook, and the worshippers in Christchurch.

Our psalm teaches us that God is always present with us. Inescapable. When I heard the story about the caretaker, I wondered. What was his job description? Did it include confronting a man in the act of killing persons who worshipped in the building? I suspect not. And yet, that is what he did.

He was a caretaker. When persons were in prayer on Friday, which is a holy day to Muslims, they were bowed down to the floor. Quite unable to protect themselves or see danger. But the caretaker was there. When he heard shots fired, he leaped into action.

Care for others is at the very heart of our humanity. Without it, none of us would be alive today, sitting in this sanctuary. We are here because someone took care of us. Care for others is also the very heart of God.

We are God's image-bearers. Fearfully and wonderfully made. Intricately woven together in the depths of the earth. All our days numbered when none of them yet existed. All those children in Sandy Hook who were slain were fearfully and wonderfully made. Intricately woven together in the depths of the earth. All the hairs on their heads counted. Children of God.

All the persons gathered to worship on Friday in Christchurch were fearfully and wonderfully made. Intricately woven together in the depths of the earth. All their days numbered when none of them yet existed. All the hairs on their heads counted. Children of God.

But there is more to this beautiful psalm than these words. There are also these: "O that you would kill the wicked, O God, and that the bloodthirsty would depart from me . . . Those who speak of you maliciously. Those that lift themselves up against you for evil! Do I not hate those who hate you, O Lord, and do I not loathe those who rise up against you? I hate them with perfect hatred. I count them as my enemies" (Ps 139:19–22).

Can you hear these words echo in the mosques filled with persons bowing to the floor in prayer as shots rang out? Can you listen to the rage in these words? Is not anyone who cuts down persons who are bowed down in prayer an enemy of God? Is this not evil?

Yes. Yes, it is. And if we have seen too many tragedies to feel it, we need to tear open our hearts and let it sink in. All of it. But this is not the psalmist's last word. The last word is a prayer for guidance. "Search me and know my heart. Try me and know my thoughts. See if there is any wicked way in me. And lead me in the way everlasting" (Ps 139:23-24).

Scripture teaches us that "'Vengeance is mine, I will repay,' says the Lord" (Rom 12:19). We are not to take vengeance and violate God's precious human life. And thank God for that. Left to our own devices, we would surely end up doing the very things we hate.

So, what are we to do? We are to care for one another. We are to be a caretaker. The man who finally stopped the violence rushed in with nothing in his hands and grabbed on to the shooter with all his might. Chased him away with his own gun.

Today, I challenge you to be a caretaker. Caretakers are fierce people. Just try to get between them and the people they love and protect. A lion and her cub. A mother and her baby. The job isn't pretty. It's gritty and gutsy and courageous. And it usually doesn't involve rushing into a room full of violence.

Usually it takes the form of tiny choices we make each day. Choices to love. Choices to remember. Choices to hold up the Muslims among us, who will suffer even more because a senseless violent act took place halfway around the world.

What did we say to ourselves six years ago when the children were killed at Sandy Hook? That it would never happen again? We must do more. And what we need to do may turn out to be harder than rushing into a room full of violence.

Ask yourself today: What would it take to stop this? Let God search your heart, lead you on the right path, and send you the fire of the Holy Spirit so you can stand. Don't let those children, and these people, and all the others, die in vain. Be a caretaker. By the grace of God, be a caretaker. Amen.

Looking back on my long struggle to find a way to act and speak into our polarized world with a gospel word of challenge and hope, I can see what I needed to do wasn't so much to preach about social justice but to demonstrate it in my own life. While the church did not choose to follow me into all the places that journey took me, they were able to see my life, gather courage from my actions, and occasionally join me in the struggle.

Does anyone know what happens to a sermon? A sermon should always lead to change. Sometimes the sermon changes the preacher. Sometimes the sermon changes the persons who hear it. While a sermon may be uplifting and informative, even transformative for the life of a preacher or listener, a sermon should always lead to action. God's word is transforming, always accomplishing God's purposes. A sermon reaches its goal when God's people act in ways that demonstrate the presence of God's kingdom on earth. The life of Jesus teaches all of us, including preachers, that such action is not always well-received. It can even be dangerous. But to whom do we owe our life? Is it not to God? And who does God want us to serve? The powerful? The wealthy? The successful? No. God wants us to serve the poor. The church is instructed to proclaim the gospel, "even at the risk of losing its own life."[2] Such service is a journey of suffering love; a journey that never ends.

---

2. *Book of Order of the Presbyterian Church-USA*, F-1.0301

# CHAPTER THIRTEEN

# "In Our End is Our Beginning"[1]

I DECIDED TO LEAVE the role of a pastor in full-time ministry in January 2019, when I was on retreat at Holy Wisdom Monastery. I called Morgan and he told me he had fallen twice during the holidays. No damage done, but a warning: "If you want us to write this book together, we'd better get to it!"

My aunt had issued a similar warning to me the year before: "Karen, if you're going to write that book with Morgan you'd better hurry up. He's past ninety, you know!"

During my many years of ministry, I believed the same God who had called me to pastoral ministry would also call me to depart from it. I wouldn't be left to wander in the wilderness and wonder if my time in a church was coming to an end. I would know. I would be called again. Called to a new journey.

I struggled with the question of retirement for over two years, rolling the question back and forth in my mind. But when I had that conversation with Morgan while on retreat at Holy Wisdom, I knew I was being called again. A sense of deep certainty and clarity settled over me. But in the weeks that followed that decision, I second-guessed that decision over and over. I had been employed in a job since I was fifteen. I didn't know any other way to live. What would happen to me? Would there be anything for me to do,

1. Sleeth, "In the Bulb There is a Flower," 250.

anywhere to go? Was this the end of the line? Although I was fretful about this big change that was approaching, I also came to realize that transitions can be very fruitful.

I began to mentally prepare for my departure. As I did this, I also began to visualize my leaving in the eyes of the congregation, recognizing what they might need, what questions they might have, and what tasks remained to be completed. The work of preparing them also prepared me, as I found answers to my own questions too.

On the Sunday after Easter, I told the session about my retirement. The announcement was made to the congregation the following Sunday. The response of the congregation was muted at first. I had to remind myself I had been thinking about this for over four months, while they were just hearing about it. Gradually, as the weeks passed, people began to speak to me about my leaving.

During the nine weeks after I announced my departure, I received more sermon feedback than I had received in the previous ten years! One young man from my confirmation class told me he couldn't imagine listening to another preacher, and he shook my hand! Others spoke of how much they appreciated my speaking to them face to face. They spoke of the personal stories I had shared and of the times they felt like a sermon had spoken to them personally. "Just what I needed to hear that day." Persons who wanted more social justice in sermons said they finally heard what they had been waiting for. The congregation also told me my sermons were more relaxed and better than any they had heard from me before.

I knew these were my last days, my last moments to share with them. I cherished the last time I took communion to persons who could not come to church. The last new member we received. The last baptism. The last sermon. And even the last session meeting! It was time for my lips to sing and my heart to open, and my eyes to cry. No time for holding back now. I was struggling mightily with the grief of separation, worries about what would become of me after I stopped being a pastor, and doubts about the future. But when I could focus on what the congregation needed to hear in those days, I was freed from those struggles. In these last days we had together, the sweet fruit of God's blessings and grace surrounded us, lifted us up, and strengthened us. I was reminded of Paul's thorn, the one he begged God to remove three times. The Lord said to him, "My grace is sufficient for you, for power is made perfect in weakness" (2 Cor 12:8–9). Here is one of the first sermons I preached after announcing my retirement:

## SERMON: A GREAT CLOUD OF WITNESSES

I was sitting in Evanshire Presbyterian Church on my ordination day. Friends, pastors from the Chicago Presbytery, and members of my home church were there. Morgan, my friend and mentor, was the last one to speak in the service. He gave the charge; the last words of blessing spoken before I would depart into the paths of ministry.

He began with a story. As he was arriving at a hotel while traveling, he saw a family packing up their car. Their little boy was delighting himself with a toy sword that he was using to wipe out all the villains in the parking lot. When it was time for him to get into the car, his father scooped him up and put him on his shoulder. The little boy continued to wave his plastic sword, slaying all the enemies. Oblivious to the shoulders that held him up.

Remember, Morgan said, we all sit on the shoulders of others. As you battle evil and proclaim the gospel, remember. The lives of centuries of faithful people have put you where you are today. You sit on their shoulders. Their witness supports you.

The first sermon I ever preached was a sermon on Hebrews 12. Two weeks before I left for seminary, my pastor Colette told me I could preach at my home church. I already knew what passage I would choose. I had listened to those words of Hebrews in my heart for months. "Therefore, since we are surrounded by so great a cloud of witnesses, let us run with perseverance the race that is set before us, fixing our eyes on Christ, the author and finisher of our faith who for the joy of the prize set before him, endured the cross, forsaking its shame, and is now seated at the right hand of the throne of God." (Heb 12:1–2)

I was an untested, middle-aged woman embarking on a brand-new journey. Before I left, I wanted to try my hand at this thing called preaching. After that first sermon, my pastor told me I would eventually learn not to put all my knowledge into a single sermon. My boss commented on my verse-by-verse approach. Do preachers still preach like that? A bit humbling, that first sermon.

Hebrews describes the journey of faith as a long-distance race. It is not the kind of race most of us think it will be. If I wanted to run a marathon, I would know what to expect. I would know the distance, know the course, know what would be demanded of me.

But the journey of faith? We do not know the length of it. We do not know the challenges, the obstacles, the things that will stop us in our tracks. The things that will break our hearts, drive us to despair and threaten to do us in.

There are two things we must remember in the journey of faith. The first is to fix our eyes on Christ. He is always going ahead of us. All the circumstances that clutter, cling, tear away our certainty—we must turn from them and fix our eyes on Christ. That is the biggest lesson ministry has taught me.

The second lesson I have learned is to graciously receive the help of others. Let myself sit on their shoulders. The love of others has rescued me from spiritual disaster many times. People like all of you have taught me to stop trying to be in charge or self-sufficient. You have been patient teachers of this pastor of yours. And I am so thankful for you.

In these days when I approach retirement, I find myself back at the place where I started. T. S. Eliot said it best: "We shall not cease from exploration, and the end of all our exploring will be to arrive where we started and know the place for the first time."[2] On the brink of this new journey of retirement, I am reminded of the days before seminary, days when I couldn't see what was ahead.

2. Eliot, *Four Quartets,* loc. 728 of 748.

I have an aunt who has cared for her handicapped son for all the decades of her adult life, and who also cared for her husband through many illnesses. A few weeks ago, she sent an email to the whole family. Her son was afraid no one would remember his birthday. So, we all, probably dozens of us, sent him a special birthday message. Many years ago, when her husband was having a spell of bad days, she would send out a family missive: "Send well wishes!!"

We need each other. But we are not alone. We are also surrounded by a great cloud of witnesses. You have been part of my great cloud of witnesses these many years. And I am so grateful. Amen.

## MORGAN'S RESPONSE

Good sermon! And I'm sure you realize that I love any sermon that mentions me. Yes, I remember that ordination service and the story that I told. Your recollection of your first sermon and how you put all your knowledge into it is so interesting—and you've come so far since then.

The most powerful lesson that you deliver in this sermon is your realization that you sit upon the shoulders of the people of your congregation—that they are a great cloud of witnesses cheering you onward. Many pastors never realize how much they are carried by the common folks of their congregation. When that happens, they never really connect with the hearts of their people because they have become entertainers. What has always been clear to me is that you've never become such an entertainer (and it's a temptation when we learn to deliver our sermons without the aid of a manuscript). You are concluding your ministry on a high note. Keep up the good work! And by the way, Happy Birthday ahead of time! Just think, when you were born, I was in my first year of seminary!

Morgan

A few weeks after my retirement announcement, the congregation and I had a difficult conversation about homosexuality. I had struggled with preaching about this issue during all my days of ministry. But now, as I faced those final Sundays, I knew I must send a clearer message. The sermon I preached was titled, "The Blessing of Diversity." I felt I still hadn't been as forthright as I had hoped. I never found the boldness to preach like Paul, but I found the courage to say what I felt God needed me to say that day. That sermon was written the week before I preached it. It was the only last-minute sermon I preached during my years of mentoring with Morgan. I learned years ago on the Sunday after Sandy Hook that an important event the congregation has experienced during the week deserves the time and effort of writing a sermon last minute. This one was so last minute, I didn't have a chance to send it to Morgan.

## SERMON: THE BLESSING OF DIVERSITY[3]

The service began with a drum call. I was in the chapel of Louisville Seminary, at the inauguration of our new President in April. The African drums echoed each other, a contrapuntal conversation. In ancient times, villages did not have ways to call a meeting. The villages were far away from each other. So, when it was time to worship God, the call to worship was sent with the sound of drums. The rhythms were communication, a sort of Morse code, telling each village the meeting would happen. As the drum call continued, the faculty and esteemed persons came down the center aisle, bedecked in colorful robes, stoles, and hoods of many colors, reflecting their degree, and where they had earned that degree.

I served on the Presidential search committee at Louisville Seminary for almost two years, and this night was a celebration of all our hard work. Our tenth President was an African American man from Howard

---

3. Sermon video on mentoringwithmorgan.com/resources/.

University, and he came with a message: "Whosoever: A Divine Invitation."

In ancient times, before the call of Abraham, the sons of Noah scattered in different parts of the earth, adopting different languages. In Genesis 11, we find a story that comments on that scattering. This year, I share this story with you as a prelude to Pentecost. Next week, we will hear the story of how the Holy Spirit came to the gathered disciples on the festival day of Shavuot. People from all over the earth had gathered, and when the spirit came, they each heard the gospel in their own language. The disciples were speaking the languages of all the gathered people with the help of the Holy Spirit.

Unlike Pentecost, the story of Babel is a disturbing story. It tells of a time when all the people were in one place, shared one language, and sought protection in a building of their own making. God scattered the people from that place, and diverse languages, cultures, and tribes populated the earth.

Why would God do such a thing? The way I learned the story, I was told the people were proud and powerful, and God wanted to punish them for building a tower and making a name for themselves. But now, years later, I wonder. I am taking a second look.

Could it be that God favors diversity over homogeneity? That God wished that humankind develop differences? When I first started studying birds and bird behavior, I was struck with the sheer number of bird species. They all have different calls, different behavior, different migration patterns. Why did there need to be so many birds? Wouldn't one bird be enough to cover the bird category?

God didn't think so. Our creation is populated with tens of thousands of different birds. Different trees. Different beasts of the sea and land and air. As Annie Dillard has said, "The Creator loves pizazz."[4]

Sizes, shapes, aptitudes, colors, lifestyles, cultures, languages—humankind is a vast array, a demonstration of our joyful, creative God. But the story of Babel teaches

4. Dillard, *Pilgrim at Tinker Creek*, 139.

us that we do not always welcome all these differences. The people in Babel wanted to keep things the same. Huddle together away from that strange diverse world God created and retreat into the sameness of one language, lifestyle, and culture.

Our world testifies that humankind is still reluctant to move out of our tower comfort zones. When we called Alton Pollard, our first African American President, one of the questions the search committee asked itself was, "Are we ready for Alton?"

Alton had a history of standing against injustice in all its forms. He was eloquent and vocal and most of all, he was unafraid. We knew some might be offended by him.

But then the question: If not now, when? How long will we wait to extend the "Whosoever" invitation? To place our fears of diversity aside and embrace the creation that God has set before us?

During all my years of ministry, I have heard the cry for unity in congregations and denominations. We want to be united. But what kind of unity does God desire? The story of Babel tells us that unity in sameness is not what God has in mind. All our efforts to smooth over our differences by trying to erect a tower of sameness will fail.

The only unity that can come to us is through embracing our differences. Cultures, genders, languages, races, sexual orientation, political views—these things are reflections of our diversity. Jesus offers the divine embrace of grace to each one of us. "For God so loved the world, that he sent his only begotten son, that whosoever believes in him will not perish but have everlasting life" (John 3:16).

Whosoever includes me! Thanks be to God! Whosoever includes each one of you! And whosoever includes the precious young adults we recognize today, whose handicaps the world would like to turn away from. These students we recognize today with our gift are children of God. Created in the image of God. Beloved. Accepted. Loved. In God's creation, no one is left behind, no one goes down the drain, no one is unclean. We are all accepted, just as we are. And that, my friends, is the best news in our whole wide world. Differences open bridges of understanding, binding us together as God's people and giving us the only unity that lasts.

Whosoever will may come! Amen.

As I headed into the final stretch of ministry, Morgan's replies reassured me during those difficult days of saying goodbye. His words of blessing were passed from my heart to the hearts of the people in the congregation. The congregation and I were having parallel experiences. We were asking ourselves the same questions. What are we going to do now? What's next? The specter of separation stirred deep anxieties. More than ever, I found myself preaching words I needed to hear myself. Two weeks before I left, I sought refuge in one of my favorite Scripture stories: the story of Elijah's flight to Mt. Horeb.

## SERMON: WORK TO DO[5]

On my last day of work as the Director of Quality Management at the hospital where I had worked for eighteen years, I dressed up like a clown. I wore an orange wig, large blue shoes, a red nose, and a clown suit. When I stopped for gas on the way to the hospital, a child leaned out the window of a car passing by, pointed at me, and exclaimed to his mother, "Mom, it's a clown!" I dressed like a clown that day because it was the only way I could manage going to work on my last day. I went from floor to floor greeting my nursing friends, saying goodbye for the last time. Then I stopped by the President's office. He motioned me in. "I hope you don't take this personally, but quality just isn't that important anymore." When I heard this, I walked out the door, glad I had chosen to be a clown on my last day.

As I look back on that last day at the hospital, I realize now that my leaving there was the beginning of a new life. But if you would have asked me what I thought at the

5. Sermon video on mentoringwithmorgan.com/resources/.

time, I would have probably told you it was the end of my career. When I experience the world crashing in on me, I sometimes jump to dramatic conclusions.

So did Elijah. Elijah was a bona fide hero of faith. He was faithful, confident, and authoritative. Able to bring about miracles through prayer, even raising the dead and calling fire down from heaven. He faced off 450 prophets of the pagan god Baal to demonstrate that the God of Israel was the one, true God. He then slayed all of Baal's prophets. When Jezebel heard her prophets were all slain, she set out to kill Elijah.

Elijah ran for his life. He was on the road for forty days and forty nights before he finally took shelter in a cave. Totally worn out. Sleeping a lot. Complaining a lot. Suicidal. He had to be told to eat. His view of reality was distorted. He was quick to blame others for the situation in which he had found himself. Had he walked into a mental health clinic he would have been diagnosed with major depression.

Despite his magnificent victory on Mt. Carmel, there was no final victory for Elijah or his God. The oppressive system endured; it didn't implode. Despite his valiant effort, he was now running for his life. It had all come to nothing.

But God wasn't done with him yet. God beckoned Elijah to the opening of the cave so he could see God as God passed by. Elijah might have been expecting a showing like the one experienced by Moses: wind, fire, and earthquake. Indeed, Elijah did see a mighty wind, fire, and an earthquake. But God was not in the mighty wind. God was not in the fire. God was not in the earthquake.

What next? Only the sound of sheer silence. So still. So small. Elijah knew. He wrapped his mantle around his face before going out because he was afraid to see God. But God simply asked him what he was doing there. Then Elijah launched into his litany. He was no better than his ancestors. He was the only one left who was faithful. He was ready to die.

I remember that before leaving the hospital, a friend told me that everyone can be replaced. No one is so spectacularly special that the place couldn't function without her. I shook that comment off. But today, I know it is true. I really believed in those days that I couldn't be replaced. I really believed that I could be greater than the ancestors of persons who had come before me. I really believed I stood alone. I was a lot like Elijah.

None of that was true, for Elijah or for me. And despite my grandiosity in thinking I was more special than anyone else, I didn't get a divine rebuke. Neither did Elijah. Instead, God set him straight on a few things. There were still several thousand faithful Israelites that had not bowed down to the pagan gods. He had never been alone. And there was going to be a future for him beyond the cave. A humbler future, but an important future.

It wouldn't be a future where Elijah would continue his victorious performances and put an end to Jezebel. That job would fall to somebody else. His future would be more like an eerie calm. And his job would be to pass the mantle, enact the relatively unspectacular act of prophetic succession. Elijah still had work to do. His work was to recognize that he wasn't the only one who would secure Israel's future and God's reputation. He needed to anoint another prophet and another king.

After leaving the hospital, I tried my hand at climbing more spectacular career heights by becoming a consultant. But God was not in the windy place of consulting. Then I tried my hand at self-sufficient self-employment. But God wasn't in that stormy place, either. God was in a quiet, but insistent voice that led me to the humble work of being a pastor.

And now, God is calling me to the even-more-humble work of being retired and giving the rest of my life away to others in some fashion yet-to-be-determined. Writing a book with a beloved teacher and friend. Giving my hours to speaking for others, caring for those others are too busy to notice. Learning to notice the stillness and sink deep into God's presence there.

God's words to Elijah—and to me—are, "You are not alone. I care for you. There is still work for you to do. Now get back to it." Not spectacular words, but words that fit. I pass those words on to you, because they might fit for you, too.

You are not alone. Others will care for you, as I have.
There is still work to do. Now get back to it.
Amen.

## MORGAN'S RESPONSE

After reading your opening story and the scripture lesson, I wasn't sure where this sermon was going. I can
remember sermons upon this text, but I can't remember
one that saw what you have seen in the passage. You begin by noting that no one is irreplaceable. Somehow or
other, the world (or the church) will find a way to go on
without us. What is more important is that, even when
it seems we've come to an end of our life's work, there
is still work that we are being called to do—but it won't
be like before. It will be like an "eerie calm," quiet and
unspectacular.

I wonder if this is not true for every life. I wonder
if God's program for each one of us is, finally, to enter
into the eternal silence where, unnoticed by the world,
God works through us in deeper, quieter, more powerful
ways—even though no one will realize what is being accomplished by our silent faithfulness. I wonder if it's as
though our final calling is to live in a hidden hermitage,
into the healing silence of which we prayerfully bring
our neighbors (those whom God brings to us every day),
holding them quietly before God. It's almost spooky how
this sermon connects with my present experience. The
other day I wrote in my daily journal, "Your true life is
in the keen, bracing air of those silent mountains where
God is known. It is a secret life that need not be made
known to others. A hidden hermitage is your real home,
in the solitude of which you live a life of simplicity, fast-
ing, and prayer. Into this mountain monastery you bring
your neighbors, though they may not know it. There, in
the great silences, the immortal diamond of their true
self is held quietly before God. This is your life now until,
someday, you will disappear and walk cheerfully into
eternal Spring."

After I had written these words, we received a call from an unlikely source, a young lesbian neighbor who was seeking "prayer warriors" for a friend who was in a terrible accident. I would never have known that this young neighbor would be seeking someone who had time for the unnoticed work of intercession. Is this the hidden life to which God is calling all of us? If so, it gives an entirely new meaning to what, otherwise, we have been calling retirement. These are the reflections that this sermon has awakened in me. So, thanks.

Morgan

## MY RESPONSE TO MORGAN

Wow, Morgan, this is powerful stuff! Makes me believe even more in the importance of writing the book! The journey of talking about sermons has led both of us to this place of greater humility. How did that happen . . . or is this just the endpoint of all journeys? I am convinced that all our connections with others, and with God, are very deep and very active; even in our cellphone world. Your neighbor who had no apparent connection to you or your devotional life was led to you. The time we have spent learning together has shown both of us just how important human contact is. You may be on your way to a hermitage . . . but you will not be alone there.

My last sermon at First Presbyterian carried with it a story from my life of those last days before leaving, a life of unpacking and repacking. All the disruption and tying up loose ends, all the mourning every last time I would do the things pastors do, brought some genuine surprises. One of those surprises happened on a Saturday night when I lost my ordination certificate at the very moment it became important to me! When I found the ordination certificate, I also found a copy of the words Morgan spoke to me on the day I was ordained.

## SERMON: ALWAYS REMEMBERED[6]

The pastor from a church in Pittsburgh told me a story of a graduate student from Scotland who joined his Presbyterian church while he was in college. After he joined, his mother in Scotland sent the minister a booklet that had been published when their church celebrated one of its anniversaries. At the back of the booklet, there was the customary list of pastors who had served that church since it had been established. The pastors who served the past two centuries were listed with full titles like Rev. Dr., but as the list went on the titles became simpler, just Rev. John Stewart. They had the names of only five pastors who served before the Reformation. At the bottom of the list was the earliest record, the name of a pastor who served in the year 1226. There was no title, not even a last name. All it said was "Richard-1226." Richard, the name with which he was baptized.

This is a day of remembering and saying goodbye. In times of remembering and saying goodbye, it is good to be reminded of God's love for us. Some time ago, my mother began to lose her ability to remember. Eventually, she forgot the sentence she had just spoken. "Did I tell you . . . ?" she would say. I would simply say, "Yes, Mom, you did." Then she would tell it to me again. One night, when I was staying overnight in her apartment and we went to bed, she called out to me from the other room, "Karen, did I remember to feed you today?" "Yes, Mom, you did."

During those years of caring for Mom, Psalm 139 was a pillar of comfort and strength for me. It tells me of a God who has always known me and known all of me. A God who knows me only as Karen. A God who also knew Mom and was holding her close.

Even when *our* memory fades, God remembers us. The one who laid the foundation of the earth formed each one of us, knit us together in our mother's womb, and numbered all our days before none of them yet

---

6. Video on mentoringiwithmorgan.com.

existed. When memory fails, God's steadfast love carries us like a mother carries a child.

And how does God remember us? God remembers us like that last citation in the anniversary booklet of that church in Scotland: Richard—1226. Karen—2019. God remembers us by name. God remembers us the way we were on the day we were baptized. Newly born in the image of God. A child of God. God's memory of us does not fade as we age. It is not tarnished by the mistakes we have made or the bitter lessons we have learned. To God we are just a babe, looking out at the world for the first time. A babe who needs to be held, fed, cared for and loved. A babe that makes everyone smile. She hasn't even done anything yet! Proven herself! Even remembered her own name. Yet God loves her.

I get a sense of that beautiful child God sees when I have visited the old and dying. One morning several years ago, after being told one of our members, Hal, was having a difficult day remembering things, I visited him with some of you and watched his eyes light up across the room when we walked in. He remembered us! He saw love in our eyes, and he recognized it. As he did, I could see the face of a little boy named Hal when his father returned home from work or when his mother surprised him with a birthday gift. That little boy face was shining through more and more the closer and closer he neared the end of his journey.

Last week, I had my own memory crisis. While moving my belongings from the church to the house, something horrible happened. I couldn't find my ordination certificate! It was Saturday night and I hadn't studied my sermon for Sunday morning, and here I was, leaping from room to room, looking through stacks of paper over and over.

Finally, I gave up and headed for the church, thinking it was there. As I drove, I remembered something. A single box I brought home the first day of moving. I told myself I was going to put that box in a very special place. It was so very special, I spent two hours trying to find it! Back safe at home, holding my ordination certificate close to my heart, I wondered. What was so very special about this piece of paper?

Then I remembered the day I sat in the pew of my home church and was told, "Don't lose your dreams. Don't give up on taking risks or cease to trust in the power of kindness and peace. These belong only to you and to God. They are who you are."

Today I say these same things to you. Don't give up your dreams of bringing God's kingdom to earth, however dark the days become or how small a change your efforts bring. Don't give up on taking risks, even when the risks seem great. We are disciples of one who risked everything.

And finally, remember to greet the one who will come after me to lead you like you like you greeted me. Cast your loving eyes upon him and listen, just as you did with me.

At the end of every service we have a benediction. A benediction is a blessing. Today, this sermon has a benediction, too. It is my blessing for you:

"Rejoice in the Lord always, and again I say rejoice! Let your gentleness be known to everyone. The Lord is near. Do not worry about anything, but in everything by prayer and supplication with thanksgiving, let your requests be made know to God. And the peace of God, which surpasses all understanding, will guard your hearts and minds in Christ Jesus. Finally, whatever is true, whatever is honorable, whatever is just, whatever is commendable, if there is any excellence or anything worthy of praise, think on these things." (Phil 4:4–8)

Amen.

## MORGAN'S RESPONSE

It is interesting that, in your final sermon, you've uttered some truths that have spoken so profoundly to me. "Richard 1226" was such a piercing reminder that, finally, that's all that will be remembered—"Morgan 1953"—or some other date along the way at some other

church. In the end, I will be almost totally forgotten. Those who knew me during the years of my pastorate will be replaced by others who never knew me. And even if the details of my ministry are recorded in some anniversary booklet, that written record will, sooner or later, gather dust on a shelf. The degrees or honors I've accumulated along my journey, the physical buildings or financial accomplishments to which I gave leadership and would wish to be remembered—all of that will be gone and forgotten. All that will matter is that my way of life touched some heart, that some kind word made all the difference, that some sermon helped someone to breathe more easily, that some smile lifted some heavy heart, that some wordless action helped someone in distress—those are the real accomplishments that will have been carried into heaven and acknowledged when I leave this present world and meet those souls again. Such little moments of daily ministry that any child of God can make possible on any and every day are the stuff of eternal substance, the only agenda that matters as we begin every new day. Anyway, thanks for another fine sermon!
Morgan.

The sermon story about Richard—1226 that opened the last sermon I preached at First Presbyterian was a story Morgan told at my ordination service some fifteen years before. I discovered that story when the words Morgan spoke that day "fell out" of the ordination certificate my last week as pastor when I opened its dusty cover. When I opened that piece of paper, I found the words Morgan spoke to me at the very beginning of my ministry. They were words of blessing.

The other story I discovered in that ordination service was the story of the little boy waving his sword while being carried. I was surprised to discover that in the original story Morgan told, the little boy wasn't carried on the shoulders of his father but carried by his mother. Also, the little boy wasn't still waving his sword, battling enemies. He was tired and he was letting his sword dangle by his side as his mother carried him.

The story of the little boy was something I heard in Morgan's blessing that was so important I not only used it several times (you probably remember hearing it more than once in this book), but I also changed it so it fit different sets of circumstances. It was the kind of story that families tell. A story that has a deep essential truth, but the details are changed as the generations tell it again and again.

So, what is the essential truth in this story that was part of Morgan's blessing as I set out on the journey of ministry? First, it is a story of a child. And, indeed, no matter how old we become, or how experiences change us, we always remain a child. Next it is a story about battle. Our lives always engage us in some form of battle. The battle to journey into our deepest self, the battle against evil, the battle to hold back the darkness or build a bridge across the breach of anguish, pain, or death. But soon, we find we cannot travel that journey or fight that battle alone. So finally, it is a story of being carried. Sometimes it is on shoulders so we can see beyond the fray. Sometimes it is in arms when we are too weary to go on. My journey with Morgan of fifteen years is a series of stories that spring from this taproot story of our shared humanity. A child, engaged in the battle life holds, is sometimes carried to see what lies beyond, or sometimes simply rests in strong, warm arms.

But why did I change that story of a child being carried by her mother, sword dangling at her side to a story of a child being carried on the shoulders of her father, waving her sword boldly in the face of her enemies? I suspect that at the beginning of ministry, I couldn't embrace the story of a tired child being carried by her mother from the field of battle. Such an image was too scary for an untested pastor who felt she was ready to tread the paths angels feared to tread. That untested pastor wanted the story to have her securely on the shoulders of a another and able to see what lay ahead.

But at journey's end, the original story was still waiting for me, tucked securely inside my ordination certificate. Still echoing silently in my heart. Yes, I was securely held on shoulders. Morgan's shoulders, and the shoulders of countless others who "happened to show up," just in the nick of time. Yes, I could sometimes see far ahead into the distance. But more often, I needed to be carried in someone's arms, too tired to wave my sword or slay demons. I was just another child of God who needed to be carried the rest of the way home.

So, here are the original words Morgan spoke. Words that became the flesh and bone of my life in ministry, and a blessing to all the people I served.

## AN ORDINATION CHARGE

Karen, I remember the day of your arrival on our campus. I could never have guessed back then how many hours we would spend together in our weekly supervisory sessions, how you would become a part of our family, sitting often at our family table. Neither could I have imagined how you would ripen as an effective preacher, with a genuine pastor's heart, who will lead her people with the same gentle, shepherding spirit. It is a special honor to be invited to be a part of this service, which is being held in your home church. You have told me of the many ways in which the pastor and people of this church have been a part of your call to ministry, and of how they have prayed for you and supported you from the beginning.

I have wanted to have an opportunity to deliver this charge for almost a year. I jotted these thoughts down early one morning in the first week of October of last year, hoping that someone at some time might ask me to deliver a charge at their ordination, and it turns out that you have become that someone. These thoughts did not come to me in an inspiring place; it was not at all the kind of place in which preachers get sermon ideas. For that matter, it was not a place where we even wanted to be. It was just that we couldn't drive any farther on the previous day, and so had checked into a downtown motel in the western town of Carson City, Nevada, where the main street was lined with the glaring and garish lights of gambling casinos. It was the worst night of our month-long western motoring trip. We got up early to get away as soon as possible.

As I packed the van, I watched a young family walking across the parking lot. There was a young father, holding the hand of a six-year-old girl, and a young mother, leading a three-year-old boy. I watched the little boy with fascination; he was evidently headed into battle, wearing the red cape of medieval warrior, and brandishing a long plastic sword. It was not clear whether he was going to engage an army or a dragon, but he was prepared to do battle. For some reason, however, as they neared the door of the breakfast room, from which many strangers were emerging, this tiny warrior turned to his mother and asked to be carried. And so, he was carried into battle in the safety of his mommy's arms, still wearing his red cape, with his sword dangling behind.

Try to hold on to that picture, Karen, because it is the best image that I can offer you for a strong entrance into your ministry. I say that for two reasons:

Don't ever put away your sword.

Don't ever let go of the youthful dream of slaying dragons.

Now you well know that many students who enter our seminaries nowadays can hardly be called youthful. It's not like it was in the old days when most of my generation came to seminary right out of college.

Nowadays, most arrive with valuable previous professional experience—and I think that our churches will be better served by those of you who have had such previous experience. Still, whatever one's age, hardly any student answers the call to ministry without having had some sort of bright, energizing vision, some dream about setting out upon a mission that will make a difference, make the world a better place. Anyone who ever accomplishes anything in ministry will never do so without some vision of doing battle with the powers of darkness. So, just don't ever let go of the dream of slaying dragons.

But it's not easy to hold on to a dream. The long years of ministry can wear warriors down. When I returned to the 40th reunion of my Princeton Seminary class of 1953, some of my classmates had left parish ministry to serve other important ministries in the world. I admired them for the courage that it took to change course. Others arrived in a state of sheer battle fatigue, wearing the honorable scars of combat in those days of the civil rights struggle. I admired them for their bravery. Whatever the future years of ministry may bring for you, Karen, don't ever lose that sense of being engaged in a battle that matters.

Albert Schweitzer once described such a loss of our first dreams as a kind of "resigned reasonableness."[7] It takes place when we abandon our earliest ideals. To steer more safely through the perils of life, we lighten our boat, tossing overboard as unnecessary ballast precious goods we once deemed indispensable. But as we do this, what we are dumping is the very food and drink that sustains our souls. When we give up believing that it is worth taking risks to speak out for truth and justice, when we cease to trust in the power of kindness and peaceableness, something goes hollow at the very center of our souls. While we pretend that nothing has happened, complimenting ourselves upon having mellowed and matured, what has happened is that we have lost our vital center. As C.S. Lewis once noted, we think that we have found our place in the world, when all along, the world has found its place in us.[8]

The important thing is to understand the many fields of action upon which the battle for God's kingdom is being waged. Be sure to tend your own soul, and to do battle with your own inner demons. Many faithful ministers have suffered burnout while waging war on the hot-button issues. When they discovered that those campaigns could not be completed in one lifetime, they collapsed with fatigue because they had not fought the interior battles that must be won to keep oneself alive and well for the long haul.

Obviously, there are large, major justice issues in which we must be engaged. But just as vital are those little unnoticed issues of pastoral care. It matters that you tend your flock, taking time to give individual attention to each soul. Always remember that souls take priority

7. Schweitzer, *Reverence for Life*, 125.

8. Lewis, *Screwtape Letters*, 20.

over statistics, and that persons are more important than numbers.

It matters that you be informed and vitally engaged in the mission of the church, as that mission is pursued in your presbytery. If necessary, be willing to raise a lone prophetic voice, but also remember Reinhold Niebuhr's advice: "Nothing we do, no matter how virtuous, can be accomplished alone."[9]

At every moment of your ministry, you are touching many more lives than you realize and making a difference in those lives. At every moment, your efforts are being complemented by the work of many other faithful disciples, so that, even if you cannot measure your success, the combined faithfulness of many disciples is carrying the kingdom forward a few more inches.

Most of all, remember that, on whatever front the battle is joined, at every moment of your life and ministry, you are helping or hindering the advancement of God's kingdom. Indeed, every tiny, seemingly mundane moment of your life has meaning for your ministry. Every small act of goodness, every little word of kindness, including the moments when you resist the temptation to speak an angry word or harbor a hateful, resentful thought—everything matters and advances God's kingdom of love and justice. The most infinitesimal moments of goodness, while wholly unnoticed by others, are known to God. And because God knows every effort you make to be faithful in ministry, be assured that your labor is never in vain.

So, don't ever put away your sword. Don't ever let go of the youthful dream of slaying dragons. But also, don't forget that, just like that little boy, you are always being carried into battle.

Indeed, you have been carried all along, carried since the day of your baptism. There's something that will always be more important than your ordination. While it may seem shocking for me to tell you this after you have endured three years of seminary and, after that, standard ordination exams, I must tell you that the most

9. Niebuhr, *Irony of American History*, 63.

important event in your life occurred many years ago at your baptism. Yes, rejoice in this day of ordination. But prize as the greatest gift the day of your baptism. If you remember that, you will always stay closer to your people. It will remind you that you are, like them, just one more little child of God, saved by grace, and carried moment by moment in the arms of your Shepherd.

My church in Pittsburgh had an extensive campus ministry. While many students participated in worship and in our college programs, very few affiliated as members. I will always remember one graduate student from Scotland who did become a member. After he joined, his mother in Scotland sent me a booklet that had been published when their church celebrated one of its anniversaries.

At the back of the booklet, there was the customary list of pastors who had served the church since it was established. However, this list was interestingly different. The names of the pastors were listed in two columns to distinguish between those who had served before and those who had served after the Protestant Reformation.

The pastors who had served during the past two centuries were listed with full titles as, The Rev. Dr. James McTavish, D.D, LL.D. But as the list went on the titles became simpler, just Rev. John Stewart. While they had evidence to prove that their church had been in existence for more than 1,000 years, they had the names of only five pastors who had served before the Reformation. Finally, at the bottom of the list was the earliest record, the name of a pastor who was serving in the year 1226. There was no title, not even a last name. All it said was "Richard—1226." All that was left was the name with which he was baptized.

Sooner or later, except for a few who get canonized as saints, the many ministers and officers of a church are forgotten. We become a faded photograph on a hallway wall or a brief paragraph in a misplaced anniversary booklet—and after a very long time, maybe not even that. Finally, however, it will not matter that on earth we were a "Reverend" or a "D.D." or a "D.Min." or a deacon or an elder. What will matter is that we were simply the children of God's covenant, just like all the other little children of God throughout the centuries, in many different times and places.

Wield the sword of the Spirit; slay dragons, Karen. But remember that you are always being carried by God's grace as a child of the covenant.

When I read that charge again, after hearing it fifteen years ago, I was stunned by how much it reflected the months and years that lay ahead. How much, unseen, those initial words of blessing were played out in the grit and joys of each day I spent as a minister. How much they also reflected my journey to become a better preacher.

The young child held in her mother's arms, her sword dangling behind. The dragons that must be slain as a servant of God is brought face to face with the evils that try to stop us, muzzle us, or rob us of any hope of making a difference in the world, until we finally look away from those dragons and see the faces of those who are being crushed by them, take heart, and continue the battle.

The loneliness of ministry as we stand alone in front Sunday after Sunday, proclaiming there is still good news. Good news! The temptation to try to do things all by ourselves because it is so much harder to involve others. The arrogance that waits around the corner of every success. The despair that waits around the corner of every failure. The temptation to forget who we are, the failure to remember we belong to God, not to ourselves. The struggle with every breath to trust God in all things.

As I continue in new journeys, I take Morgan's blessing with me. And through this book, I also share that blessing with you, dear reader. I close with words Morgan shared with me many years ago: "So let me draw you to the great forgiveness. Not as one who stands above you, but as one who says, 'I, too, was poisoned with the flowers that sting, but now, forgiven, I am toiling up the road to heaven. Rise, and let us face these heights together!'"[10]

10. Weatherhead, *When the Lamp Flickers*, 42.

## CHAPTER FIFTEEN

# The Power of Blessing

THE DAY I WALKED into the office of Morgan Roberts and saw his bald head hiding behind a large computer screen, I never imagined the journey that lay ahead of us, never imagined Morgan's first words, "You must free yourself from the manuscript." The painful searching for how to remember the sermon instead of wandering in the wilderness, waiting to find my way back and make a safe landing. Learning that the kingdom of God cannot be found behind a pulpit, but instead in the road of daily life.

In 2003, at the beginning of our mentoring relationship, I hung on every word Morgan spoke. I only slowly began to find my own voice, my own preaching style, and my own truth. The back-and-forth of mentoring, the "third room" in which the give-and-take of insights is shared, produced more than just a better sermon—it produced concrete actions that changed some part of the world and the realization of what we pray weekly: "Thy kingdom come, Thy will be done on earth as it is in heaven" (Matt 6:10).

As the journey continued, I began to realize Morgan was not only helping me, I was helping Morgan. My best effort of the week became fodder for his creative mind and generous heart. He would often email me with the words, "In the middle of the night, I woke up and was thinking about part of your sermon." Throughout our years together, Morgan never failed to emphasize the importance of communicating face to face, eye to eye, heart to heart—the sincere conversation of the Christ in me to the Christ in each person to whom I spoke.

While he was reviewing manuscripts of this book, Morgan sent me the following story:

> During my Pittsburgh ministry, when a young couple in my church was removing old carpeting in their home, they discovered that old newspapers had been used for padding under the carpeting. One of the papers from the 1920s was the Saturday edition of the local newspaper. What was fascinating was that the page advertising movies and entertainment faced the page listing church worship services. It was as though one page offered Saturday night entertainment, while the facing page listed Sunday morning entertainment. It was sad commentary upon the paper's understanding of church worship.
>
> But, has anything changed? Judging by comments that I hear frequently, many church-going people still judge worship by entertainment factors. Did the preacher hold my attention? Was the sermon interesting? Was the sermon too long? Was the music pleasing and appropriate? Of course, such comments are made with the supposition that Sunday worship should be "inspiring." But inspiring to what? Do those who are "inspired" leave worship determined to save the world in some way? Of course, we never know what happens until we hear of some daring and adventurous application of the sermon being made by some worshipper. Hopefully, this is what should happen to sermons, and this is what we believe mentoring relationships can foster.

So, what will you take away from our book? If you are beginning in ministry (or some other vocation), will you seek a mentor? If you are an older, seasoned, or retired member of your guild, will you offer yourself as a mentor to someone? If you are a seminary professor or administrator, will you consider setting up some system that matches young graduates with older alums who could be helpful mentors? These are the challenges with which we leave you.

Wherever you find yourself in your journey, Morgan and I will welcome some communication from you (Karen at: kbrugler1@ comcast.net or Morgan at: mrob1928@gmail.com). Neither of us are now mounting a pulpit every Sunday, seeking to say some good word for Jesus. Instead, we're out on the road where he is. That's where he was first seen in Luke's account, as the Emmaus disciples say, "Were not our hearts burning within us while he was talking to us on the road . . .?" (Luke 24:32). Christ still walks on our road today, and we hope we'll see you sometimes on that same road.

# Bibliography

Ball, Deborah. "Pope Francis Sees Limits to Freedom of Speech." *Wall Street Journal.* January 15, 2015. https://www.wsj.com/articles/pope-francis-sees-limits-to-freedom-of-speech-1421325757#:~:text=MANILA%E2%80%94Pope%20 Francis%20waded%20into%20the%20debate%20over%20freedom,faiths%20 can%20expect%20to%20provoke%20a%20strong%E2%80%94even%20 violent%E2%80%94response.

Barker, Margaret. *Lost Prophet: The Book of Enoch and its Influence on Christianity.* Sheffield: Sheffield Phoenix, 2005.

Barth, Karl. *The Word of God and the Word of Man.* Translated by Douglas Horton, 1928. Digital ed. London: Hodder and Stroughton, 2017.

Baxter, Richard. *Reformed Pastor.* Edinburgh: Banner of Truth Trust, 1974.

Bellinger, Karla. *Connecting Pulpit and Pew: Breaking Open the Conversation about Catholic Preaching.* Collegeville, MN: Liturgical, 2014.

Berry, Wendell. *What are People For?: Essays.* Berkeley: Counterpoint, 2010.

*Book of Order of the Presbyterian Church-USA* 2019–2021. Louisville: Westminster John Knox, 2019.

Broadus, John Albert. *Treatise on the Preparation and Delivery of Sermons.* New York: Armstrong & Son, 1887.

Buttrick, George, ed. *The Interpreter's Bible, Volume 7.* 12 vols. New York: Abingdon, 1951.

Buttrick, George. *Preaching Jesus Christ: An Exercise in Homiletic Theology.* Philadelphia: Fortress, 1988.

Dillard, Annie. *Pilgrim at Tinker Creek.* New York: Harper Perennial Modern Classics. 1998.

Drummond, Henry. *The Greatest Thing in the World.* Grand Rapids: Baker, 2011.

Eliot, T. S. *Four Quartets: Little Gidding.* New York: Houghton Mifflin Harcourt, 1971.

Esquivel, Julie. *Threatened by Resurrection: Prayers and Poems from an Exiled Guatemalan.* Translated by Ann Woehrie. Elgin, IL: Brethren, 1980.

Gaarden, Marianne. *The Third Room of Preaching: The Sermon, the Listener, and the Creation of Meaning*. Louisville: Westminster John Knox, 2017. Kindle edition.

Kierkegaard, Soren. *Purity of Heart is to Will One Thing*. Start Publishing, 2012.

Lewis, C. S. *The Screwtape Letters*. New York: Macmillan, 1961.

Macartney, Clarence E. *Preaching Without Notes*. Eugene, OR: Wipf and Stock, 2008.

MacDonald, George, *The Gospel in George MacDonald*. New York: Plough, 2016.

Niebuhr, Reinhold. *The Irony of American History*, Chicago: University of Chicago Press, 2008.

Predmore, John, SJ. "Poem: On Bliss by Paul Claudel." *Ignatian Spirituality: Go Set the World on Fire* (blog) https://predmore.blogspot.com/2010/04/poem-on-bliss-by-paul-claudel.html#:~:text=Poem%3A%20On%20Bliss%20by%20Paul%20Claudel.%20There%20is,which%20deprived%20of%20daylight%2C%20worships%20in%20the%20night.

Pritchard, J. B., ed. *Ancient Near Eastern Texts Relating to the Old Testament*. 3rd ed. Princeton: Princeton University Press, 1969.

Raven, Charles E. *The Wanderer's Way*. New York: Henry Holt, 1929.

Schweitzer, Albert. *Reverence for Life: The Words of Albert Schweitzer*. Anna Maria, FL: Maurice Bassett, 1993.

Sleeth, Natalie. "In the Bulb There is a Flower." *Glory to God*, 250. Louisville: Westminster John Knox, 2013.

Stagg, Frank. *The Book of Acts: The Early Struggle for an Unhindered Gospel*. Nashville: Broadman, 1955.

Thompson, Dean, and Cameron Murchison, eds. *Mentoring: Biblical, Theological, and Practical Perspectives*. Grand Rapids: Eerdmans, 2018.

Thurman, Howard. "The Sound of the Genuine." Edited by Jo Moore Stewart. *The Spelman Messenger* 96.4 (Summer 1980) 14–15.

Weatherhead, Leslie D. *When the Lamp Flickers*. Nashville: Abingdon, 1948.

Wesley, Charles. "Love Divine, All Loves Excelling." *Glory to God*, 366. Louisville: Westminster John Knox, 2013.

Wiman, Christian. *Every Riven Thing*. New York: Farrar, Straus, Giroux, 2010.